34.95

X

Government Grief

Government Grief

How to Help Your Small Business Survive Mindless Regulation, Political Corruption, and Red Tape

Amy H. Handlin

 PRAEGER

AN IMPRINT OF ABC-CLIO, LLC
Santa Barbara, California • Denver, Colorado • Oxford, England

Library of Congress Cataloging-in-Publication Data

Handlin, Amy H., 1956–
    Government grief : how to help your small business survive mindless regulation, political corruption and red tape / Amy H. Handlin.
        p. cm.
    Includes bibliographical references and index.
    ISBN 978–0–313–39259–7 (hardback) — ISBN 978–0–313–39260–3 (ebook)
1. Small business—Government policy—United States. 2. Trade regulation—United States. 3. Bureaucracy—United States.
I. Title.
HD2346.U5H375   2011
658.1'20973—dc22   2011010797

ISBN: 978–0–313–39259–7
EISBN: 978–0–313–39260–3

15 14 13 12 11   1 2 3 4 5

This book is also available on the World Wide Web as an eBook.
Visit www.abc-clio.com for details.

Praeger
An Imprint of ABC-CLIO, LLC

ABC-CLIO, LLC
130 Cremona Drive, P.O. Box 1911
Santa Barbara, California 93116-1911

This book is printed on acid-free paper ∞

Manufactured in the United States of America

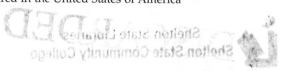

To David, Daniel, and Rebecca

Contents

Introduction

Knowledge Is Power

Business leaders recognize that knowing your market is a key to success. They will not make a move without research and analysis. But when dealing with government, many of these same smart businesspeople strike out blindly, trying to beat a system they do not understand. Some feel intimidated by official pomposity, even—or especially—in their own backyard. Many get frustrated or confused by Byzantine procedures. But all make a fundamental mistake: they fail to appreciate that in government no less than in business, knowledge is power.

Businesspeople who are knowledgeable about government can pinpoint who is likely to help them—and who is not. They are experienced and shrewd about when to speak up, and how. When approaching officials, they anticipate opposing points of view and are prepared to compete in the marketplace of facts and opinions. Even when their efforts fall short, they open doors and create opportunities for the future.

But if you are not part of this government-savvy group, you have plenty of company. Most small businesspeople have, at one time or another, given up in the face of mindless regulation, political corruption, or red tape. You may have decided it just isn't worth your time to try to push back. That is not unreasonable when you're on your own. Time is money, and it is tedious to amass the necessary information and insight.

But you are no longer on your own. This book will give you the knowledge you need: in one place, in jargon-free language, and always with a small businessperson's perspective in mind. Although you might continue to abhor government officials, institutions, or processes after reading and using this material, you will never again feel powerless to deal with them.

A HATE-LOVE RELATIONSHIP

> The nine most terrifying words in the English language are: 'I'm from the government and I'm here to help.'
>
> —Ronald Reagan

Government is easy to hate. Just ask a few disgruntled businesspeople, like these:

- The Dallas developer whose three-year, 11,000-square-foot office/retail project was approved by multiple city inspectors every step of the way, then denied a final certificate of occupancy. None of the officials who had scrutinized the building had noticed that it was 15 feet too close to the street.[1]
- The owners of a South Carolina retail funeral store who filed their paperwork, paid for their license, and got a green light to open their doors ahead of a routine appearance before the State Board of Funeral Directors. As soon as they started selling caskets, they were slapped with a $1,500 fine for "opening before their Board appointment."[2]
- The Boston merchants victimized by a crooked state senator who demanded cash bribes in return for permits and licenses. A surveillance camera caught her stuffing the $100 bills into her bra.[3]
- The New York businessman who was forced to fight water bills from the city—and repeated threats for nonpayment—for a building he had demolished four years earlier.[4]

Even those without personal horror stories have clearly been influenced by disgruntled acquaintances. Businesspeople routinely believe that government is designed to make their lives as costly and frustrating as possible. Based on a decade of tracking entrepreneurs' opinions, pollster John Zogby put it simply: " 'Small business owners normally fear and loathe the government.' "[5]

They are not alone. One national study found that 70 percent of Americans believe "Government creates more problems than it solves."[6] In another survey, only 4 percent of respondents expressed "a lot of confidence" in government's ability to solve problems. Large numbers agreed that "Government is incompetent."[7]

But the realities of the government-business relationship are more complicated. Undeniably, some public agencies seem to have more than their share of foot-dragging or incompetent bureaucrats. At the same time, the help of others is essential to small firms competing with limited resources in a tough economy.

It is easy to forget that government creates and maintains the most basic building blocks for business growth. These include a vast infrastructure of transportation, sanitation, and education facilities; a judicial system to protect commercial and property rights; and a stable money supply. None of these functions perfectly in twenty-first-century America, but in their absence—say, without highways, public schools, criminal prosecution, or orderly procedures for dispute resolution—our modern market economy would rapidly disintegrate into a primitive, lawless, chaotic free-for-all. Moreover, government-sponsored scientific and technological research continually spins off private-sector opportunities in fields like biotechnology, energy, and communications. Government testing and review bolster consumer confidence in the safety of products as diverse as food, cribs and pharmaceuticals.

Crises jog memories. During the economic collapse of 2008 and 2009, businesspeople all over the country implored government to solve problems ranging from unscrupulous debt collection to predatory advertising. States and towns not only cracked down on such wrong-doing, but in many cases took the initiative to go further, devising new ways to support local enterprise with credit counseling, management training, investment incentives, mortgage guarantees, utility assistance, and much more. Officials recognized that even so mundane a fixture as a beefed-up public library could become a critical resource for free employment, marketing, and financial data.

These efforts did not go unnoticed. In a national small business survey conducted during the most painful part of the recession, nearly three-quarters of respondents said they would recommend their city to other businesses. Far from viewing town hall as a den of thieves or idiots, "The majority of small businesses are looking to their local governments to help them succeed," commented the pollster.[8]

The idea of a business-friendly government may seem counterintuitive, but it is not new. A 1997 story in *Business Week*—with the unlikely headline "When Bureaucrats Are a Boon"—concluded:

> Hard to believe, perhaps, but with perseverance, any smart small business owner can get a leg up on the competition or help solving a problem by turning to government. No, that's not an oxymoron. That's good business.[9]

THE FEAR FACTOR

Whether or not small businesspeople recognize that government is not all bad, relatively few take advantage of opportunities to question, challenge, or even learn how they can benefit from government. According to the National Federation of Independent Business, the majority of small employers make no effort to contact public officials about legislative or regulatory matters that powerfully affect them. "Given the strong views small business owners seem to possess about government's impact on their operations, the lack of contact is surprising. Perhaps there is none because they expect no helpful response from it," suggested NFIB. The problem has been noted by others: In testimony before Congress in 2004, the chief economist for the Small Business Survival Committee cited "the fear factor" as a key stumbling block for employers who might otherwise speak up.[10]

Even if they are not exactly afraid, small businesspeople clearly feel uncomfortable and ineffectual when they do initiate contact with government. Although many studies document this widespread frustration, it takes little more than a call to any local chamber of commerce to find evidence of it. Scholars call the feeling "low political efficacy"—a lack of confidence in one's ability to change anything. But research also shows that when people build their competence and self-confidence in dealing with government, they are more likely "to secure a response from government officials, even when those officials generally are unresponsive to the demands of other citizens. . . . In other words, a belief in oneself as an effective political actor may be a necessary condition for the mobilization of political discontent."[11] Again, knowledge is power.

Academic propositions aside, the reality is straightforward. You have no chance to overcome mindless regulations, political corruption, and red tape if you do not even try. In fact, it is a self-fulfilling prophecy: Convince yourself that the bureaucrats will always win, and they will. By reading this book, you can overcome the fear factor, build self-confidence and learn to combat frustration with information. You will give yourself a viable alternative to pessimism, cynicism, and defeatism—often understandable when dealing with government, but rarely constructive.

REALITY CHECKS

Few small businesses will generate a fortune overnight. Similarly, it is rare for a one-time interaction with government—a single email, an isolated phone call—to produce significant results. To avoid getting discouraged—and to budget sufficient time for your effort—it is important to begin with realistic expectations of what lies ahead. Here are six basic reality checks:

(1) Almost always, you will need a plan. Striking out blindly—showing up in random offices, yelling at any staff in sight—will be about as effective in a government building as in a jungle. Set aside the time you will need to choose the most appropriate target and develop a smart, persuasive approach.

(2) Your first plan may fail, sometimes for reasons beyond your control. If so, do not waste time railing against stupid bureaucrats—fine-tune your efforts and try again. Often, persistence and diligence can make up for minor missteps.

(3) Even if you are an accomplished multitasker in your business, don't expect this skill to work for you when dealing with government. One step at a time, pinpoint exactly what you need to know and to do—based on the structure of this book—and tackle the challenges individually.

(4) Everywhere in the much-maligned bureaucracy, expect to encounter creative solutions. Be open to new ideas, no matter how unlikely the source.

(5) Whatever the merits of your argument, and whomever you encounter in government, you have the right to expect professionalism and certain basic courtesies. Do not hesitate to insist on:
    – Undivided attention and respect
    – Clarification of confusing terms, forms, or processes
    – Access to a person, not just a voicemail
    – Complete, comprehensible answers to reasonable questions
    – Information provided in writing on request
    – Explanation of all complaint and appeal mechanisms
    – Identification (by name and title) of individuals who interact with you, and their bosses
    – Documentation of every current and potential cost of your transaction
    – Patience and politeness

(6) The most important reality check of all: Don't court disappointment by expecting government to act like a business. Although it is realistic to hope that the public sector will increasingly adopt some fundamental industry practices—like cutting spending when revenues drop—it is a fool's errand to seek corporate managers at the statehouse. That is not because of ignorance about the economy, or hostility toward business. It is simply because (for better or worse) government was never designed to turn a profit, but to accomplish tasks deemed necessary for the public good. Public institutions must be fair to all citizens, while

private industry maximizes returns to a few—its investors, customers, employees, and other stakeholders.

There is no excuse for government activities or requirements that are wasteful, unethical, pointless, harmful, or counterproductive. But for perspective, it is useful to remember that bureaucratic bungling not infrequently afflicts the private sector, too. As acknowledged by one business writer:

> This idiocy can occur anywhere. At a Chicago deli we were told, "Take a number." "But there's no line," we said. "Rules are rules," the clerk said, shrugging.[12]

THE FOCUS OF THIS BOOK: STATE AND LOCAL GOVERNMENT

Firms of all sizes are affected by every level of government. But in comparison to large corporations, small businesses are far more vulnerable to the actions of officials in their own backyard. That is why most of the guidance in this book has a state and local emphasis.

Let's say your town decides to shrink the allowable size of restaurant signs: under the new regulations, your mom-and-pop sandwich shop will barely get noticed on a street with dozens of big-name competitors. The change will hardly register with national chain eateries, which have enough brand recognition and advertising prowess to overcome signage problems in any one location. But it could cost you several orders per day—the difference between profit and loss.

If you are a local contractor, your firm could be devastated by so-called "impact fees," charges imposed on every new structure built in a community to fund roads, parks, schools, and other public improvements. Authorized by legislation in about 22 states, then enacted at the discretion of counties or towns in those states, impact fees can be circumvented by national builders with the ability to shift their operations to friendlier jurisdictions. But as a hometown business, you cannot escape this hit to your bottom line.

Imagine being a small landlord in a town widely acknowledged— even if only in whispers—to be rife with political corruption. Do you live in fear of a shakedown? Set aside cash for payoffs? What do you tell prospective tenants worried about "the crooks at city hall"?

Of course, the fact that small businesses suffer disproportionately from local government grief does not mean they are insulated from Washington. A neighborhood convenience store must comply with nearly as many federal government rules as a multinational corporation.

In fact, the compliance costs for small firms are 45 percent higher than for their larger competitors. This is a hidden—and strikingly regressive—tax that can kill jobs, increase consumer prices, and lower incomes.

To voice problems with onerous rules, big companies routinely hire big-time lobbyists. But it is a rare small businessperson who can pay such pricey professionals, or sacrifice the time and money necessary to travel to the U.S. Capitol. As a practical matter, most must work through intermediaries—for example, staff at a state or local business development center—who can muster federal contacts and expertise to get answers, provide help, or run interference.

State and local officials are far more accessible than their counterparts in Washington, and more susceptible to pressure from their constituents. This is not to suggest that small businesses are completely shut out of federal agencies—in Section II of the book you will learn about e-opportunities and other ways to directly address them. But if you have limited time to invest in your dealings with government, you will get the highest return on that investment by staying close to home. The director of your town's environmental commission, for instance, will be more responsive to your needs than anyone in the U.S. Environmental Protection Agency—if only because she knows you will keep coming back (and complaining to the mayor) until you are satisfied.

Moreover, hometown officials and their staffs can readily marshal and coordinate resources from other sectors of government. In a growing number of localities, small businesses can access one-stop information shops expressly designed to help them navigate the maze of regulations, programs, and opportunities. There are many variations. For example, Albuquerque's Economic Development Department partners with the U.S. Commerce Department to access expert advice in international certifications and global supply chains. Kansas City, Missouri, created a "Bizcare Customer Service Center" to provide information, referrals, troubleshooting, and advocacy—along with open-access city hall computers. More examples are discussed in Chapter Five. But whatever their characteristics, what most of these facilities have in common is underutilization. Too many who could benefit from them don't know they exist, largely because they never asked.

Whether or not they know about nearby services to help them, small businesspeople are keenly aware that state and local government can hurt them. In a 2007 nationwide survey of entrepreneurs, the majority agreed—by a wide margin—that state and local laws affect them more than federal policies.[13] The National Small Business Poll came to the same conclusion from another direction: Its respondents reported that they contact state and local officials to complain or seek help far more often than they reach out to Washington.[14] Those interactions— government grief at its most personal—are the focus of this book.

HOW TO USE THIS BOOK

This book is organized into two broad sections: *What You Need to Know* and *What You Need to Do*. Begin by skimming both sections to get a sense of how they complement and build on each other.

Section I will help you understand the big picture. Why is the government bureaucracy so big? Who invents regulations? How do crooked officials hurt your business? Do local politics matter? The clearer your view of this landscape, the more easily you will be able to navigate it.

Look for the mini-case studies called *Tales from the Dark Side*. These real-world vignettes are eyebrow-raising and often entertaining, but they serve a more serious purpose: to illustrate key structural or administrative flaws in government.

Here is a *Tale* that shows how well-intentioned regulations can have unintended, and sometimes nonsensical, consequences.

Tales from the Dark Side: A Distasteful Requirement

In an attempt to help specialty beer and liquor stores, legislators in Maine passed a law allowing the stores to offer the same kinds of taste testings that had boosted the revenues of wine shops. However, the law also required liquor retailers to prevent children from observing adults while they imbibed.

This forced small stores and those with windows to rig elaborate shields, creating a furtive atmosphere more conducive to jokes than sales. As one owner described her makeshift barrier: "She has to cover her front and back door windows with black and drape a sheet across the large storefront windows, giving her shop the feel of a 'speakeasy' during her monthly tastings."[15]

Section II will teach you how to confront regulatory and other problems yourself. Chapters Five and Six discuss an array of research and targeting skills, both basic and advanced. Chapters Seven and Eight explain how, when, and why to speak up—even if your reasonable requests are stonewalled.

In this section, you will find brief items titled *Tips and Techniques*. Here is an example:

> If you need to visit several government offices, it can be mind-boggling just to keep track of names and job titles. But you should make a special effort to get each individual's direct email address. Otherwise, your follow-up communication will disappear into a general office mailbox— the cyber-equivalent of a black hole. There is no way of knowing how often that mailbox gets checked, or by whom.

This book is designed to help readers with different kinds of issues and varying levels of experience (good or bad) in dealing with government. It is not necessary to read the chapters in the order they appear, or in equal detail. For instance, if you have a regulatory problem but understand the administrative rulemaking process, you could skim or even skip Chapter Two—but pay particular attention to Section II, which will help you target, refine, and amplify your efforts to influence that process. If you are experienced in gathering public documents, Chapter Five might be too basic for your needs—but you can still learn advanced research techniques in Chapter Six. Are you confident there is no corruption in your city? Although few municipal governments are pure as the driven snow, Chapter Four will be less immediately useful than other material.

But the operative word is *immediately*. Information that seems irrelevant or superfluous today could jump out at you tomorrow. For example, you may have been successful in the past using one communication tool, like emails, but now find yourself in need of another, like testifying at a public hearing. Also, whatever your level of expertise, the examples, approaches, and perspectives throughout the book can refresh your ideas and deepen your insights.

Take some time to familiarize yourself with the model communications in the Appendix. Instead of starting from scratch, in most cases you will be able to adapt these materials to your own needs.

A real language barrier exists between government and citizens— sometimes, even between officials themselves. So make use of the glossary. You will save time and avoid confusion by learning some of the lingo.

Most importantly, lose no time in getting started. Do not hesitate or procrastinate. When dealing with government, a solid effort can splinter on the rocks of unforeseen—and often very tight—deadlines for applications, appeals, and other documents. Recognize that officials who are juggling many different problems every day will not recall the details of your situation if you allow weeks or months to elapse before reminding them.

The bottom line is that waiting will get you nothing but more government grief. Reading this book will get you results.

KEY POINTS TO REMEMBER

- Learning how to engage constructively with government is more than a defense—it can help you compete with limited resources in a tough economy.
- The more you build your competence and self-confidence in dealing with government, the more likely you are to get the right results.
- State and local officials are far more accessible to small businesses than their counterparts in Washington, and more susceptible to pressure from their constituents.
- No matter how challenging your problem with government: Don't hesitate, procrastinate, or give up.

NOTES

1. R. Bush, "Zoning Error Stalls Building Project, Devastates Developer," *Dallas Morning News*, November 1, 2007, dallasnews.com.

2. Office of Governor Mark Sanford, "Governor Signs Bill for Better Hair," May 14, 2008, scgovernor.com/newsrelease.

3. M. Viser, J. Drake, M. Levenson, J. Saltzman, and A. Ryan, "Wilkerson Vows to Stay in Race, Criticizes US Attorney," *Boston Globe*, October 29, 2008, boston.com.

4. S. Malanga, "Small Businesses to NYC: Get Off Our Backs!," *City Journal*, Autumn 2009, p. 7.

5. J. Zogby, quoted in R. McGill Murphy, "Who Will Win the Entrepreneurial Vote?," *Fortune Small Business*, September 25, 2007, CNNMoney.com.

6. D. Bok, *The Trouble With Government* (Cambridge, MA: Harvard University Press, 2002), p. 43.

7. J. Weisberg, *In Defense of Government* (New York: Scribner, 1996), p. 32.

8. R. Elmore-Yalch, quoted in "Small Businesses Want Local Government Support in the Form of Tax Breaks, Fewer Regulations" Opinion Research Corporation, Princeton NJ, June 15, 2009, www.opinionresearch.com.

9. C. Farrell, "When Bureaucrats Are a Boon," *Business Week*, September 1, 1997, www.businessweek.com.

10. R. Keating, "The Government Regulatory Burden on Small Businesses," testimony to Congress on behalf of the SBSC, April 22, 2004, www.sbecouncil.org.

11. S. Craig and M. Maggiotto, "Measuring Political Efficacy," *Political Methodology* 8 (1982): 3, 86.

12. W. Peck and W. Casey, "Resist Efforts to Run Business Like the Government," *Denver Business Journal*, April 25, 2003, denver.bizjournals.com.

13. R. Murphy, "State and Local Laws Affect Small Business Owners More Than Federal Ones," *Fortune Small Business*, September 25, 2007, CNNMoney .com.

14. National Small Business Poll, National Federation of Independent Business Research Foundation, 3 no. 1, 2003, www.nfib.com

15. Quoted in K. Miller, "Lawmakers Want to Amend Wine Tasting Law," *Bangor Daily News*, November 9, 2009, www.bangordailynews.com.

Part I

What You Need to Know

1

Red Tape Rising

OVERVIEW

In the private sector, business cycles act as a natural brake on workforce expansion. When times are tough, companies downsize and outsource to shrink the size of their payrolls. Hiring accelerates when business picks up.

But government consistently breaks the rules of boom-and-bust. Not only are there no significant reductions in public sector employment when the economy turns sour, but typically, the number of bureaucrats goes up even as business revenue goes down. More functionaries means more balkanization of government, increasingly complex public entities and, of course, spiraling red tape.

This chapter explains why.

Section 1: How We Got Here

The historical perspective is instructive: Today's frustrating bureaucracy was yesterday's inspiring innovation.

Section 2: Citizen Expectations

The number and quality of today's public services would have been inconceivable for much of the last century. As citizens have received more, they have also come to expect more from every level of government. It is hard to say no.

Section 3: Government Inefficiency

You've heard the old joke. Question: How many government bureaucrats does it take to change a light bulb? Answer: One to change it and four to fill out the paperwork.

Although the reality is not (always) that bad, it is woefully close.

Section 4: How Government Creates More Government

No matter how laudable the purpose, federal grants to the states—and from the states to counties and towns—almost always mean new public jobs, increased fragmentation of government, and more red tape.

Section 5: Lobbying for More Government

Capitol Hill swarms with hundreds of high-priced lobbyists paid with tax dollars to seek more tax dollars for their clients—states, local governments, and public institutions from colleges to sewer plants.

Section 6: Shadow Government

The quasi-public bodies known as authorities are important contributors to public health, safety, and quality of life. But they borrow and spend billions of tax dollars largely in the dark, without oversight or accountability.

Section 7: Getting Around the Runaround

Red tape will not stop rising, but you can get help cutting through it. This section tells you where to look.

* * *

SECTION 1: HOW WE GOT HERE

Government is booming. In good times and bad, in every corner of America, bureaucrats fill more jobs and wield more control over the marketplace than ever before. On a per capita basis, inflation-adjusted state and local expenditures mushroomed from about $759 in 1948 to over $4,300 per person by 2004.[1] Between 2005 and 2007, as the economy began to sputter, the number of state and local employees continued to grow by 2 percent. Over the most recent 10-year period, the state bureaucracy alone ballooned by nearly 10 percent[2]—despite revenue shortfalls and persistent calls for cuts. Why?

There are almost as many answers as there are bureaucrats. Politicians, pundits, academics, and ordinary citizens all have their own, often conflicting, opinions. But the jumble of perspectives can be sorted into three basic themes:

1. Citizens demand an increasing number of hometown government services.
2. Government is incapable of providing those services efficiently.
3. The federal government is delegating ever more responsibilities to the states—which in turn delegate to local governments and spur more county and municipal hiring and other expenditures.

None of these explanations is complete, but each is a key part of the puzzle.

Ironically, the development of a government bureaucracy was once welcomed as reform of a system driven by political patronage and riddled with corruption. Until the early twentieth century, every important public job—and many that were unimportant but lucrative—went exclusively to political allies, relatives, and friends of the politicians in power. Iron-fisted political strongmen like Chicago's "Big Bill" Thompson or Jersey City's Frank Hague dispensed, and withheld, public largesse with impunity.

County governments were no more pristine than city halls. In Nassau County, New York, longtime Republican boss Joseph Margiotta was said to control so many government jobs in the 1970s that "While (he) was chairman, some residents would call the local Republican committeeman, rather than a county agency, to get a broken streetlight fixed,"[3] reported the *New York Times* in his obituary. Like many other patronage kings, Margiotta eventually abused his power: in 1983, a kickback scheme landed him in jail.

In well-meaning attempts to get politics out of government, the administrative ranks were increasingly professionalized in the years after World War I. More and more public workers got jobs based solely on training and competence. By the mid-twentieth century, the ranks of officialdom were dominated by career functionaries, protected as well as constrained by a rigid civil service system. The hallmarks of this system—highly advanced for the time—were:

- Work performed according to detailed, impersonal rules that were difficult to bend based on favoritism or personal bias.
- Authority organized according to a clear chain of command to reduce dictatorial or subjective decision making.
- Fixed and specialized division of labor to promote the development of highly technical knowledge and skills.

Unfortunately, these "advances" led inexorably to the problems that plague twenty-first-century government: stultifying rules, baffling complexity, and narrow-minded judgments. The fact that bureaucrats once represented progress, rather than barriers to progress, is cold comfort today. But it is at least a reminder that bureaucracy was designed to advance, not thwart, the interests of ordinary citizens.

This message comes through in the observation of a management analyst during the boom decade of the 1990s, when fast-moving entre-preneurs railed constantly against the plodding pace of government:

> The government runs on rules—laws, regulations, policies and procedures—designed and developed to ensure the government serves the public interest. The people who administer these rules are thus involved in the core mission of government. There may be too many of them, some of their rules may be out of date or counter-productive, and they could probably find much better methods or processes for implementing their rules.... At their worst, they may be bean-counting, nay-saying, inflexible bureaucrats. But at their best, they are public stewards.[4]

Around the same time, Georgia citizens were asked what they thought of the service they received from government employees, like transit and postal workers, compared to staff at banks, grocery stores, fast-food restaurants, and other businesses. Far from documenting a wide gulf between bureaucrats and private providers, the survey found that average satisfaction scores were almost identical—around 74 percent on a scale of 0 to 100.[5] In a Virginia study of people's encounters with local public agencies, like the police, library, or parks department, 80 percent of participants rated their experiences either "good" or "excellent."[6]

Of course, these perspectives are meaningless if you must confront a stupid, stubborn, or uncaring bureaucrat. Or are they? In fact, the evidence shows that you shouldn't give up. More often than not, you can find someone in another office, at another time, in another setting who will not only intervene but actually become your advocate.

SECTION 2: CITIZEN EXPECTATIONS

The idea is simple. A hundred years ago, people expected, and received, little in the way of public programs or facilities. Most Americans had access to only a rudimentary system of roads and rails, a bare-bones public school, and a county courthouse. Although some wanted more, no one imagined a government that routinely built structures, provided health care, monitored commerce, even sponsored entertainment—certainly not in their backyard. Today, these are widespread, unexceptional citizen demands, and meeting them has become increasingly expensive. One rough indicator of the scope of expectations: The U.S. Census of Government Employment breaks down the basic functions of state and local workers into nearly two dozen categories. These include education, libraries, streets and highways, public welfare, hospitals, police and fire protection, natural resources, correction, social insurance, judicial and legal, utilities, and a catchall category called "other and unallocable." Moreover, as rural and suburban parts of the country have become increasingly populous and diverse, the demand for citylike service has spread to communities remote from urban life.

The bulk of the costs goes to salaries. Take parks. In 2007, over 145,000 state employees drew paychecks totaling over a half billion dollars to create, maintain, and operate various natural resources and visitor services.[7] And that's just at the statehouses. It is not uncommon for midsize municipalities—with populations under 100,000—to employ dozens of full-time parks and recreation managers, program specialists, conservationists, rangers, and maintenance crews. For example, Macon, Georgia, has a parks and recreation staff of 35 to serve about 97,000 residents. Large cities spend far more: In 2009, amidst severe budget cutbacks, Chicago's Park District was struggling to maintain a payroll of 1,700.[8]

Technology has brought steady productivity gains to American manufacturing, but there has been little carryover to the public sector because government delivers mostly services, not goods. Additionally, at least through the 1990s, wages have consistently risen faster in government than in the private sector.[9] So unless citizens scale back the number and quality of services they expect—or until policymakers defy the salary demands of public employee unions—the pattern will continue.

The widespread unionization of government workers is another key structural factor. Often layered on top of civil service protections, the due process rights and other guarantees in union contracts make it exceedingly difficult to fire, furlough, or alter the responsibilities of career public employees. A business owner with an unproductive worker need only show him or her the door. A government administrator must fill out mountains of forms, laboriously document poor performance, attend multiple hearings, and endure endless procedural delays—while continuing to sign the slacker's paycheck. Even if an incompetent worker is removed from one government job, the rules might guarantee him or her easy access to another.

The power of unions doesn't just hamstring individual administrators. Collectively, unions are a major obstacle to broader government efforts to downsize. For example, when New Jersey's governor ordered furloughs in 2009, the unions immediately challenged his executive order in court—forcing an already cash-strapped state to fund a legal defense against its own employees.

There is also the irony of supposedly nonpolitical government workers engaging in political campaigns on behalf of their unions. Union endorsements are highly coveted because they bring armies of volunteers. In some union locals, members are encouraged to "bank" paid leave hours in a pool that can be tapped for political advocacy: In other words, taxpayers pay for unions to lobby for more public jobs. New jobs generate more union dues, used in part to make hefty campaign donations, a self-perpetuating cycle of payback.

SECTION 3: GOVERNMENT INEFFICIENCY

The problem isn't just that government continually hires more functionaries to deliver more services at ever-higher salaries. It's also that government is inherently inefficient.

At least 65 studies have shown that public agencies spend more than private businesses to provide identical services.[10] Although waste and fraud sometimes play a role, this discrepancy can simply reflect a lack of competition. It can also reflect hyper-specialization. Think of the problem like a pizza maker: You will find dozens of pizza officials with authority over cheese, sauce, and crust, but no one in charge of the whole pie.

Whatever the cause, the result is the same—a bureaucracy around every corner of government that is bigger than anyone ever expects. The positive side? This fragmented decision making means that if one bureaucrat says no, there are plenty of others with the power to overrule him.

Tales from the Dark Side: The Built-In Mistake

Dallas leaders had long been eager to attract high-quality development to the city's southern sector. That's why they welcomed the proposal by a Los Angeles developer—so well regarded that his work was part of an innovative design exhibition at the Dallas Museum of Art—to erect an 11,000-square-foot office/retail building in a neighborhood badly in need of investment.

Construction took three years. A parade of inspectors from multiple city departments signed off at every stage. But when the project was tenant-ready, the builder was told that renters could not move in. Officials refused to grant a final certificate of occupancy because somehow, no one had noticed that one side of the structure was 15 feet too close to the street.

The city tried to make amends with a temporary permit, and held out hope for a waiver. But in the meantime, the developer was stuck with the costs of a vast empty space. Furious, he complained to a local newspaper about other bureaucratic snafus:

> An inspector from Building Inspection [approved] a curb that didn't include an access ramp. The city's Public Works and Transportation Department later told him part of his sidewalk would have to be ripped out so a ramp could be built. . . . Asked how one department could approve his sidewalk only to have another tell him to rip it out . . . the inspector "said we don't talk to Building Services. We don't have a good relationship with them."[11]

One reason for the persistence of inefficiency is the difficulty of quantifying it. As observed by two prominent economists:

> First, unlike private sector production, the public sector does not produce a specific number of units, but rather supplies a level of activity. As a result, this creates a monitoring problem for oversight agencies: It is difficult, if not impossible, for monitors to accurately judge the efficiency of production when no tangible or countable unit of output is

available. Second, the monopoly nature of most bureaus . . . denies funding agencies (Congress, the executive branch) comparable information on which to judge the efficiency of the bureau. Third . . . [there is] an opportunity for bureaucrats to overstate their costs in order to receive a larger budget.[12]

Even without raising the specter of dishonesty and self-aggrandizement among bureaucrats, it is obvious that costs are hard to cut when they can't be accurately measured or compared to alternatives.

Another reason is the nature of representative democracy. Simply put: Many public programs and facilities exist not because they are needed by all citizens, but because elected leaders—using the age-old tactics of horse-trading and back-scratching—fight to bring them to their districts. A determined politician who wants, say, a public health clinic can usually get it by voting for another politician's highway or school or laboratory. The question of whether or not any of those projects is cost-efficient gets lost in the politics. (On a federal level, this is known as "earmarking." Abuses of the practice—for projects like the infamous Alaskan "Bridge to Nowhere"—have spawned numerous congressional scandals.)

As the number of public employees has grown, many state and local politicians—and a not inconsiderable number of congressmen and U.S. senators—have become dependent on their votes. So it is hardly surprising that at election time, more candidates are eager to promote bigger government than significant cutbacks. Also, the most concrete way for a mayor or legislator to prove his or her support for a pet cause is to throw public money at it. As a practical matter, this brings still more jobs, whether there is a demonstrable need for them or not.

Also, public jobs have a tendency to outlive their original purpose—or any purpose at all. In a political body, it is exceedingly difficult to muster the will or the managerial discipline to weed out functions and job titles that once made sense but are now duplicative or superfluous.

The sheer number of governmental units defies any simple attempt to analyze their operations. U.S. taxpayers support approximately 88,000 public jurisdictions. These include states, counties, cities, towns, townships, independent school districts, and other entities responsible for funding and administering specialized services like irrigation, electric power, housing, or firefighting. Some states are carved into mind-boggling numbers of tiny government slivers: 6,835 in Illinois, 5,070 in Pennsylvania, 4,700 in Texas, and 4,607 in California. At a minimum, nearly every public structure employs its own administrators, secretaries, maintenance workers and, of course, tax collectors.

For example, until 2004, no one in New York's government kept a list of how many public authorities existed across the state, much less whether or not their thousands of employees were productive or necessary. These vast administrative institutions (discussed in more detail in Section 6) raised millions in taxes, tolls, and fees from New Yorkers and carried $43 billion in state-backed debt. In the state's first-ever comprehensive study of authorities, Comptroller Alan Hevesi counted 640. Many had clear responsibilities, like managing highways or running sewer plants. But the Hevesi report also identified public entities like the Mermaid Development Corporation and the Industrial Exhibit Authority—bodies so obscure that it was hard to figure out what they did (or how many people they paid to do it).[13]

Tales from the Dark Side: School Districts with No Schools

In New Jersey, the cost of public education eats up a third of the state budget and two-thirds of all property tax revenues. Burdened by the highest average property taxes in America, residents have long pressed for relief in the cost of their schools.

A logical place to start: shutting 23 school districts with school boards, administrators, and staff—but no schools. These so-called "non-operating districts" were first targeted for closure in a legislative study in 1969. But they survived for another two decades, doing little but convening meetings, maintaining records, and authorizing payments to the neighboring towns that actually educated their students, who numbered 10 or fewer in some of the districts. The Pine Valley district served five children; the Tavistock district served one. By 2006, these non-operating operations were spending over $800,000 a year. In 2004, Governor Jim McGreevey described them as "bureaucracies that oversee nothing but their own existence."

In 2009, the New Jersey legislature finally passed a proposal to eliminate all non-operating districts—though 27 legislators voted against it. The *Philadelphia Inquirer* called the new law "a small but meaningful victory against nonsense."[14]

Other inefficiencies stem from the tendency for government spending to attract more government spending—a phenomenon dubbed the "flypaper effect." Here is a simple example of how it works. Happiness County, which has never offered computer training, gets a grant from a local computer manufacturer to hire instructors who will run classes at the county library (the special problems caused when such grants come from the federal government are discussed in the next section). With great fanfare, the county commissioners launch the program with an enrollment drive. In just a few weeks, the classes fill to capacity, and everyone involved with the grant rushes to congratulate everyone else. Word spreads of the fine quality of instruction, and there are waiting lists for every available slot.

But a few years later, the computer company becomes a victim of the poor economy. It shutters its Happiness County plant, and eliminates funding for the grant. Now what? Do the instructors lose their jobs? Are the citizens on the wait lists told to seek computer courses elsewhere?

Probably not, because other jobs and expenditures are now "stuck" to the program. With increased traffic and patronage, the library has hired more staff. The county college has recruited new computer science professors. As the level of computer literacy has increased among local teens, the high schools have upgraded their software. The senior center has started a bus service to transport older enrollees. Happiness County's promotional materials and website have been revised to prominently feature all of these developments. Moreover, citizens have come to expect and depend on free computer training.

If efficiency were the only consideration, county leaders would almost certainly pull the plug on the program; they can barely afford to meet the basic transportation, safety, and public health needs of a rapidly growing population. Instead, they vote to replace the private funds with taxpayer dollars. The flypaper effect prevails.

This is not just a hypothetical or occasional phenomenon. Researchers estimate that every $100 in grants received by a local government boosts related spending by an additional $25 to $100. As noted in one review of the literature: "All studies surveyed report some degree of flypaper. The variation comes from whether the estimated flypaper effect is simply large or if it is enormous."[15] Because of competition among governments, the flypaper can even catch dollars in another jurisdiction. In other words, if Prosperity County gets jealous of Happiness County's reputation for high-tech education, it may decide to replicate the training in its own facilities.

SECTION 4: HOW GOVERNMENT CREATES MORE GOVERNMENT

The vast majority of grants to state and local government come not from the private sector, but from Capitol Hill. This creates another layer of problems and inefficiencies.

The Tenth Amendment to the U.S. Constitution sets out clear limits on the federal government, reserving most functions and powers to the states. But beginning in the late nineteenth century, decision makers in Washington turned this principle on its head. Federal champions of causes ranging from highways to agriculture realized they could simply pay the states to do what they could not—create, maintain, and expand a near-unlimited variety of public activities. In 1921, there were seven federal grant programs; today there are more than 800.

The high-profile New Deal brought huge new federal programs to the states in the 1930s. But during a lesser known boom from 1950 to 1970, the total number of these programs jumped from 68 to 530. In 1970, federal grants sent $129 billion to the states (expressed in 2007 dollars).[16] By 2008, the largesse totaled $467 billion.[17] In 2009, one expert noted that the continued growth in federal aid has "locked state budgets into programs ripe for escalating federal regulations and matching state costs."[18]

Today, this is the heart of the problem.

Three decades ago, it was already clear that Washington did the states no favors by throwing money at them. Ironically, federal analysts were the harshest critics. In a 1979 report on the aid system, the Government Accountability Office did not mince words: "[It] is an array of often conflicting activities and initiatives which defy understanding to all but the most serious students of the system. . . . Studies showed that red tape, delays, and vast amounts of paperwork were characteristics common to most . . . programs."[19] To spend the federal dollars according to rigid federal rules, state governments had created layer upon layer of new agencies, authorities, and so-called special districts—special mostly in the sense that they operated free of hometown control. Still more agencies had come into being just to figure out how states should allocate and track the millions in annual windfalls.

But instead of pulling back, national leaders decided that the best way to rein in government was with more government. In the 1980s and 1990s, with only a few exceptions, federal grants did not shrink, they simply came with more strings attached. For example, some programs began to require states to hire forecasting and planning experts, whose main function was to coordinate other forecasting and planning experts.

The most rule-bound and narrowly focused type of grants are designated as "categorical grants." Designed to control state activities ranging from road construction to acquaculture development, these are also the most plentiful. The idea is to regulate away as much state discretion as possible; in other words, to force grant recipients (states) into lockstep with grantors (federal bureaucrats). In practice, the only way to ensure this result is to create yet more bureaucracies solely for the purpose of filing documents and communicating with Washington—and, of course, cashing grant checks.

"Block grants" are structured with fewer rules and mandates than their categorical cousins. By untying the hands of local administrators, federal programs like Community Development Block Grants encourage creative responses to the infrastructure needs of small neighborhoods. But the paperwork never goes away. In typical suburban counties like New Jersey's Burlington, Somerset, and Monmouth, it is not unusual to find up to 10 full-time CDBG staff.

A tiny sample of 2010 grant programs is enough to demonstrate the reach and diversity of the federal funding web that now entangles every level of government. Many of these programs are so arcane or complex that they require specialists just to explain the rules—to other specialists whose sole function is to enforce them.

- Abandoned Mine Land Reclamation Program
- Beach Monitoring and Notification Program Implementation Grants
- Clean Diesel Grant Program
- Convicted Offender and/or Arrestee DNA Backlog Reduction Program
- Interjurisdictional Fisheries Grants
- Leaking Underground Storage Tank Trust Fund Corrective Action Program
- Pipeline Safety Program Base Grants
- Recreational Trails Program
- Refugee and Entrant Assistance Programs
- State Grants to Reimburse Operators of Small Water Systems for Training and Certification Costs[20]

If confined to the statehouses, this bureaucratic bloat would be cumbersome enough. But more and more federal programs have spilled over into city, county, and town governments, sucking up tax revenue and spewing endless red tape—rules, regulations, requirements, and policies dictating details down to the size and color of standardized forms. Why haven't local officials—a famously independent bunch—bristled at all the directives from Washington telling them what they could and couldn't do?

Look at the situation from the perspective of Mayor Smith of Pleasant Town. He has little incentive to resist federal generosity; in fact, there are at least three powerful incentives for him to do the opposite. First, the aid can pay for popular projects that Smith can take credit for without needing to fund. Second, he knows that citizens underestimate the real costs of public services not directly or explicitly charged against their tax bills—so he looks frugal. Third, as in Happiness and Prosperity Counties, there is always competition between Smith and his rivals in neighboring communities. Wide roads, classy schools, and economic development incentives, for example, can attract business investment and new residents to Pleasant Town—ratcheting up the demand for more of the same.

Another reality: When it comes to justifying the need for federal funds, state and local politicians have skin in the game. Most grants require some commitment of matching funds, which must be diverted from other uses. After the fact, how many officials will question their own judgments? Also, if the grants were used to satisfy the needs of vocal special-interest groups, their members might seek ballot-box revenge on whomever dared deny them a slice of the federal pie.

On the contrary, officials more often end up vigorously defending why and how they spent federal handouts. Especially in big public works projects, the flow of cash from Washington can be so enormous as to swamp all existing mechanisms—and motivation—for oversight. The most infamous example in recent history is Boston's Big Dig, the 15-year, $14.6-billion reconstruction of the city's downtown arteries. Although managed by the state and city, it could not have happened without an open federal checkbook. The project was plagued by mammoth cost overruns, severe engineering deficiencies, and allegations of systemic corruption. In the end, its mistakes and mismanagement turned deadly. A young woman was crushed under tons of concrete when a brand-new tunnel collapsed, setting off a sickening and fruitless orgy of finger-pointing. As one critic observed: "When every level of government is responsible for a program, experience indicates that no level of government takes responsibility when failures occur."[21]

Tales from the Dark Side: The Toilet Paper Crisis

In 2008, Detroit's troubled school system received an estimated $11,000 from city, state, and federal government to educate each of its students. But no one saw a need to efficiently direct the flow of cash, or even account for where it went.

The issue was brought to light when a principal sent letters home to parents pleading for donations of light bulbs and basic paper supplies—including toilet paper. The only apparent alternatives were to limit children's access to toilet rolls, or to institute rationing on a sheet-by-sheet basis.

Noting that public funds were "being squandered by incompetence and corruption," the *Detroit News* editorialized: "A district with a $1.2 billion operating budget should not be in the position of having to beg for supplies. The request for toilet paper and light bulbs reveals both a serious and inexcusable administration problem and a serious misallocation of resources."[22]

SECTION 5: LOBBYING FOR MORE GOVERNMENT

A major reason why government keeps growing is that you are lobbying for it.

Few taxpayers are aware that high-priced Washington lobbyists are kept on retainer by their state, county, and town governments. Still more professional advocates work for highway authorities, water utilities, public universities, school districts, and Indian tribes. Fees can range as high as $20,000 per month. According to a *New York Times* analysis, taxpayer-funded entities spent well over a half billion dollars to lobby Congress between 1998 and 2006. The target of all this pricey advocacy? The specifics vary—a town might want a bridge, a college could hope for biomedical research facilities—but the general goal is to get more of the federal funding that inevitably expands the reach and complexity of government.

In the infancy of public lobbying, a few enterprising Washington insiders drummed up business the old-fashioned way: They went door-to-door, selling states and cities the prospect of earmarked congressional appropriations and federal grants. When these efforts

---

Tales from the Dark Side: Bountiful Breakfasts

New Jersey Transit is a public agency in charge of trains, buses—and courting government funds. Over a four-year period, the entity spent over $675,000 on lobbyists. Even with one on retainer for $6,000 a month, others were hired for an additional $15,000 a month, plus expenses.

It was those expenses that caught the public's attention in 2007. As part of a bid to build support in New York for a rail tunnel between the two states, New Jersey Transit paid $200 an hour to a well-connected political insider. His primary job was to arrange meetings among officials, organizations, and opinion leaders locally and in Washington. He did so lavishly. According to a newspaper review of his bills, "On visits to Washington, Burgos regularly stayed at luxury hotels. One night at the Capitol Hilton in May cost $434. He also billed NJ Transit $462 for limousine service that he and [executive director] Warrington took to a retirement party for Warrington in March."[27]

The lobbyist was partial to morning meetings at Manhattan's posh Regency Hotel, famous for scrambling eggs for the rich and influential. These breakfasts cost taxpayers up to $60 per person[28]—at a time when New Jersey Transit was hiking train and bus fares for millions of riders.

SECTION 6: SHADOW GOVERNMENT

To finance and administer the government growth in plain sight is a vast apparatus you pay for but rarely see. This murky landscape of money and power is often dubbed a "shadow government." Its quasi-public institutions are responsible for much of the infrastructure key to the daily lives of people and businesses across America: highways, airports, bridges, waste and water treatment plants, mass transit systems, ports, dams, cargo facilities, convention centers, and more. Generally known as authorities (though sometimes called by other names like commissions or public corporations), they can be big or small, serve one town or a whole state, and run operations as diverse as television stations and race tracks. Some are simply financing mechanisms, created to issue debt and manage investments on behalf of other government entities.

But what all authorities have in common is the ability to spend tax-payer dollars with virtually no public input or oversight. Their top decision makers are almost never accountable to the voters who pay their salaries and guarantee billions of dollars in authority-issued debt. Their budgets, audits, and meeting minutes—where records exist—are obscure and typically difficult to access. Even a governor may be unable to veto or directly challenge the actions of an authority in his or her own state.

Some authorities are responsible and efficient, but others have spiraled spectacularly out of control. One example is the Massachusetts Bay Transit Authority, lead agency for the Big Dig tragedy discussed in Section 4. On the opposite coast, the State of Washington Public Power Supply System, builder of the pioneering Hanford Reactor, was put in charge of expanding nuclear power throughout the Northwest. Despite years of mistakes, delays, and runaway expenses, the WPPSS was allowed to continue borrowing and spending billions— even to authorize additional projects. Finally, its mismanagement became so egregious that WPPSS contracts were voided by the Washington Supreme Court. When the authority finally defaulted on its obligations, it had become the largest issuer of municipal bonds in America.[29]

Like many other innovations in government, public authorities were originally designed with a high-minded purpose. Early in the twentieth century, state and local governments rushed to expand in tandem with the country's rapid growth and economic development. People needed railroads, bridges, schools, and jails. But in their haste to build and inexperience with large-scale projects, many officials amassed debt so staggering that it imperiled the solvency of their communities. Others cut shady deals with corrupt or incompetent contractors. By the 1920s, there was a widespread public outcry for reform.

Authorities were invented as a means of bringing order to this chaotic infrastructure boom. The theory made sense: As in successful private firms, ownership (the public) would be separated from management (unelected and unaccountable to politicians). So as to operate more efficiently, authorities would also be freed from most of the financing and spending restrictions on state and local governments.

In practice, authorities took advantage of the easy cash but failed to resist political pressures. Supposedly independent boards and professional managers were, in fact, beholden to powerful patrons and took decisions at their behest. With few reporting or disclosure requirements, even rudimentary information about authority finances became inaccessible, or incomprehensible, to outsiders.

Today, there is increasing scrutiny of "shadow government." But fundamental change of these lumbering, secretive institutions will be a long time coming. For example, when New York's newly created Authority Budget Office reviewed the compliance of these operations with basic state laws, it found flagrant, serious violations. A third simply ignored the ABO's demands for data. In one case, budget officials notified a county development authority that its practices were not only in conflict with its own bylaws but potentially illegal. The agency responded that "the requirements of the law were viewed only as aspirational goals and not firm requirements."[30]

In the meantime, authorities continue to fuel government growth. Their role goes well beyond building public facilities.

First, these entities themselves are major employers, with a reputation for hiring based on questionable criteria. Nepotism is rampant: An audit of the West Virginia Parkway, Economic Development, and Tourism Authority found that more than 35 members of the same family were employed in one department.[31] Political affiliation routinely trumps competence, and "godfathers" often hand out six-figure jobs. For instance, at two of New Jersey's major sewerage authorities, "[A state political leader] said it's no secret the commissioners—who do the hiring at both agencies—take turns each month giving jobs out. 'Basically the patronage is done on a rotating basis, he said.' "[32] In 2010, 27 employees of New Jersey authorities were paid more than the governor.[33]

Tales from the Dark Side: Dubious Dormitories

There is nothing unusual about a state authority created to construct college housing. But New York's Dormitory Authority utilized some highly irregular business procedures.

According to a 2004 investigation by the state comptroller, the NYDA awarded a $28 million contract to a firm with less experience than other bidders. Its most important qualification to construct dormitories: the company was owned by brothers who were big-time political fundraisers. Other findings in the report were also eyebrow-raising: "Despite misrepresenting their

> qualifications and a long history of bad debts and delinquent tax payments, the company won more than $37 million in State and county contracts and subsidies."[34]

Another issue is redundancy. Many government bodies are slow to streamline operations, especially when it means shedding employees who have outlasted their usefulness; but authorities are especially notorious for looking the other way. Here is a typical snapshot:

> Look at the Pittsburgh Stadium Authority, created in the 1960s to build and manage Three Rivers Stadium. Pittsburgh demolished that facility four years ago, replacing it with twin football and baseball stadiums—built by yet another authority. Still, the old Stadium Authority lives on, an oddity that nobody paid much attention to until charges hit this summer that an authority accountant had embezzled $193,000.[35]

Authorities are advised by an unending parade of lawyers, engineers, and consultants who are in the business of facilitating ever-larger structures and operations. Once decisions are made to expand, authorities can borrow money faster and with fewer restrictions than any other public bodies. In fact, authorities nationwide issue more debt per year than any entity except the federal government.[36]

SECTION 7: GETTING AROUND THE RUNAROUND

It is a pipe dream to hope for a modern world free of bureaucracy, but it is realistic to seek help cutting through the red tape. The best place to look? Among red-tapers themselves.

This is not a new idea. In a classic 1950 essay "I Am a Bureaucrat," Oregon government worker Merrill Collett wryly acknowledged the public's disdain toward his profession. "According to both press and the Congressional Record I gormandize at the public trough. I am a spirit incarnate of sloths through the ages," he wrote. Yet, Collett argued that citizens would be better served if they could get past their distrust and "accept an occasional 'bureaucratic' recommendation. . . . Bureaucrat though I may be . . . you would be shocked at the pleasure I get from snipping red tape here, and improving a process there. For I am a taxpayer, too."[37]

Sixty years later, his thoughts are echoed by Lou Paparozzi, a 34-year veteran of New Jersey bureaucracy. "It's a mistake for people to let their cynicism get in the way of constructive engagement with government," says the former agency head and top administrator.

> If you feel like you're getting the runaround from an entry-level person, understand that it's probably because your problem doesn't fit into the 'thought box' within his purview. But you can always access higher-level bureaucrats with bigger 'boxes'—in other words, people with broader responsibilities, more experience, and enough flexibility to help you if it's possible."[38]

The nuts and bolts of this approach are discussed in Section II. For now, it is worth noting the basic philosophy. A positive attitude won't always cut through the red tape—but a disdainful attitude never helps. "I've seen it time and time again—people getting help they otherwise wouldn't have gotten, just because they didn't give up. Often in government, things can get reprioritized even when they can't be changed. The key is to connect with the people who have the authority to make it happen."

Paparozzi recognizes that bureaucrats are trained to follow rules, not to bend them. But he believes there are always some who can recast an issue from "Why is this person complaining?" to "How can this system be improved to help everyone?"

After all, better systems are in bureaucrats' interests, too. As Collett put it six decades ago: "I, the bureaucrat, [must] catch the hot potato—and hold it. There is no other receiver."

KEY POINTS TO REMEMBER

- There will always be more bureaucrats than you expect. That means more potential frustration—but also more people you can appeal to.
- When everyone is in charge, no one is in charge—except you.
- Many government operations and decisions are barely visible. But if you exert some effort, you can see them.
- It is a mistake to view all bureaucrats as enemies. Among them, you can find allies and advocates.

NOTES

1. T. Garrett and R. Rhine, "On the Size and Growth of Government," *Federal Reserve Bank of St. Louis Review* 88, no. 1 (2006): 13–30.

2. U.S. Department of Commerce, Bureau of the Census, Census of Government Employment 2005, 2007.

3. D. Hevesi, "Joseph Margiotta, Long Island GOP Leader, Dies at 81," *New York Times*, December 2, 2008, www.nytimes.com.

4. "Save the Bureaucrats (While Reinventing Them)," *Public Personnel Management* (Spring 1997), as reproduced in *Entrepreneur Magazine*, www.entrepreneur.com.

5. T. Poister and G. Henry, "Standards of Excellence: U.S. Residents Evaluations of Local Government Services," *Public Administration Review* 54, no. 2 (1994).

6. C. Goodsell, *The Case for Bureaucracy: A Public Administration Polemic.* (CQ Press: Washington DC, 2004).

7. U.S. Department of Commerce.

8. D. Mihalopoulos, "Chicago Park District Asks Employees to Take Furlough Days," *Chicago Tribune*, May 13, 2009, www.chicagotribune.com.

9. J. Ferris and E. West, "Cost Disease versus Leviathan Explanations of Rising Government Costs: An Empirical Investigation,"*Public Choice* 98, no. 3–4 (1999): 307–16.

10. D. Mueller, *Public Choice III.* (Cambridge: Cambridge University Press, Chap. 16, 2003).

11. R. Bush, "Zoning Error Stalls Building Project, Devastates Developer," *Dallas Morning News*, November 1, 2007, www.dallasnews.com.

12. Garrett and Rhine, "On the Size and Growth of Government," 22.

13. "Public Authority Reform: Reining in New York's Secret Government," report of the Office of the State Comptroller, Albany, 2004.

14. Editorial *Philadelphia Inquirer*, July 14, 2009, www.philly.com.

15. J. Hines and R. Thaler, "The Flypaper Effect," *The Journal of Economic Perspectives* 9, no. 4(1995): 219.

16. C. Edwards, "Federal Aid to the States: Historical Cause of Government Growth and Bureaucracy," *Policy Analysis* no. 593 (May 22, 2007): 1–48.

17. J. Kincaid, "State-Federal Relations: Agendas for Change and Continuity," in *The Book of the States*, 21–27 (Lexington, KY: Council on State Governments, 2009).

18. Ibid., 22.

19. General Accountability Office, "Perspectives on Intergovernmental Policy and Fiscal Relations," June 28, 1979, 8.

20. Catalog of Federal Domestic Assistance, 2010.

21. Edwards, "Federal Aid to the States: Historical Cause of Government Growth and Bureaucracy," 34.

22. Editorial, "Toilet Paper Crisis a Symbol of Larger Failure," *Detroit News*, January 14, 2009, www.detnews.com.

23. Rudoren, J. and A. Pilhofer, "Hiring Federal Lobbyists, Towns Learn Money Talks," New York Times, July 2, 2006, www.nytimes.com.

24. P. Kerpen, "Taxpayer-Funded Lobbying Fuels Big Government," *National Review,* May 24, 2007, national.review.com.

25. J. Reitmayer, "Gov. Chris Christie Says Passaic Agency Hired Lobbyists to 'Tone Down' Spending Criticism," *Newark Star-Ledger*, February 3, 2010, www.starledger.com.

26. Quoted in D. Michaels, "Hired Guns Get Hudson Rail Tunnel on Track," *The Bergen Record*, October 1, 2007, www.northjersey.com.

27. Ibid.

28. Author review of NJ Transit records, 2006–2007.

29. S. Fein, "Public Authority Controversies: Root Causes and Lessons Learned," *Government, Law and Policy Journal* 11, no. 2(2009): 35–40.

30. C. Brecher, "What Happened to Authority Reform?" *Government, Law and Policy Journal* (2009): 28.

31. W. Williams, "Turnpike Audit Shows Costs Could Be Cut," *The State Journal*, May 22, 2008, www.statejournal.com.

32. T. Sherman, "Jersey's Pipelines of Cash and Favors," *Star Ledger*, July 27, 2003, www.starledger.com.

33. A. Doblin, "Stopping the Dig, in a Chris Christie Minute," *The Bergen Record*, February 8, 2010, www.northjersey.com.

34. *Public Authority Reform: Reining in New York's Secret Government*, report of the Office of the State Comptroller, February 2004, 34, www.osc.state.ny.us.

35. C. Swope, "The Phantom of New York," *Governing*, November 2004, 4.

36. J. Rosenbloom, "Is the Private Sector Really a Model of Efficiency and Independence? Re-evaluating the Use of Public Authorities During Recessionary Times," *Government, Law and Policy Journal* (2009): 6–14.

37. M. Collett, [1950] "I Am a Bureaucrat," reprinted in *The Bureaucrat* (Winter 1983–84): 36–37.

38. L. Paparozzi, 2010, interview with author.

2

Regulatory Roulette

OVERVIEW

If regulations are the bane of your existence, you are not alone. Nor are your problems new. But regulations are not, as some believe, an immutable force of nature. Unlike storms, they can be stopped; unlike rivers, they can be reversed. Sometimes, regulatory action can be headed off before it even gets started. The key is to understand why regulations exist, how they differ, and when you can (and should) intervene in their development.

Section 1: A Perfect (Unregulated) World?

You can fight overregulation without losing sight of the need for rules to provide some stability and protect good actors from bad ones in the marketplace.

Section 2: Regulatory Roulette

The impacts of regulation can be inconsistent as well as costly. Although smart businesspeople are not afraid of risk, they resent the unpredictability of "regulatory roulette."

Section 3: The Reason for Rules

It may seem like rules exist just to frustrate businesspeople. In reality, there is no way to implement laws—whether they are good or bad for business—without some policies and guidelines.

Section 4: Your Seat at the Table

The administrative rule-making process is underutilized and little understood, but it is an open door for small businesspeople who want to influence state regulation.

Section 5: Diagnosing a Regulatory Problem

Complaining about regulation in general is not enough to change specific rules. You must learn to diagnose different regulatory problems before calling for solutions.

Section 6: Hometown Rules

Most high-profile regulatory battles focus on either Washington or the statehouse. But the stakes can be just as high at town hall.

* * *

SECTION 1: A PERFECT (UNREGULATED) WORLD?

Imagine Nirvana for small business in America. You would be free at last—no inspectors, licenses, permits, zoning restrictions, compliance reports. You could set up shop anywhere, hire anyone, advertise anything, and sell at any prices you choose. Your venture would flourish. Or would it?

Let's say you got a great deal on the old house that you have now turned into a restaurant. Then your kitchen was gutted by an electrical fire, the result of faulty wiring by a phony "electrician" who needed no license. Now you can't rebuild the damaged side of the structure, because your neighbor put a smelly dog breeding facility right on the property line. Worse, one of the dogs bit your chef when she stepped outside for a break. You don't carry workers' compensation insurance—it is not required—so she is suing for all your assets.

Your competitors see an opportunity to profit from your troubles. One runs television commercials stating that his prices are 60 percent lower and his food is 75 percent fresher than yours—lies you can't stop because there are no restrictions on advertising claims. Another uses a bait-and-switch tactic: She lures customers by promising a $5 steak which is never available, getting them to order a $30 porterhouse instead. Again, you have no recourse.

Another disaster hits: Your delivery van runs out of gas on the freeway and is smashed by a careening truck. It turns out that your driver was cheated at a gas station that filled the tank with only 20 gallons when he paid for 30—the attendant can get away with this because there is no inspection of commercial weights and measures. The truck driver was sleep deprived, but there is no federal regulation to keep him off the road.

Suddenly, your unregulated world looks less utopian than chaotic.

Whatever its contemporary merits or flaws, government oversight of business dates back to the birth of the nation. The Commerce Clause in the U.S. Constitution articulated the power of Congress to regulate interstate as well as foreign transactions. In the eighteenth century, the country's early leaders created roads, a postal service, and other parts of a nascent commercial infrastructure. Beginning with the Federal Banking Act of 1864, which laid the foundations for an orderly banking system, Washington launched a steady torrent of efforts to ensure fair competition, open communication, safe operations, trustworthy products, and ethical financial practices. They have not always succeeded: For example, price controls in most industries were largely discredited in the 1970s and 1980s. But some have played an important role in stabilizing the economy, blocking bad actors and protecting honest businesses, like yours.

What is new (or at least newer) is the mind-boggling scope of business regulation by states, counties, cities, and towns. As explained in Chapter One, this is a fallout of the steady growth and fragmentation of state and local government. It is also a product of well-meaning attempts to attract local investment and boost hometown employment.

Many rules were designed to stop abuses of power. For example, during the heyday of New York's Tammany Hall, city resources were diverted to cronies of the mayor. A Los Angeles storekeeper during the 1920s had to bribe the police for protection from organized crime—sometimes from corrupt cops themselves. The complex requirements you must meet to do business with your state were put in place to make sure contracts don't go exclusively to relatives of the governor.

Of course, regardless of why the rules exist, you cannot escape them. And in most states, the burden is likely to increase. In the spring of 2009, President Obama announced his intention to reverse a previous policy called "preemption." This restricted the ability of states to impose regulation stricter than the federal government's; any state rule on workplace safety, for example, would be "preempted" by existing U.S Occupational Safety and Health Administration (OSHA) protections. The change will mean less regulatory consistency from state to state, and more confusion for employers doing business in multiple locations. As observed by a U.S. Chamber of Commerce official: "Removing federal preemption forces employers to navigate a confusing, often contradictory patchwork quilt of 50 sets of laws and regulations."[1]

SECTION 2: REGULATORY ROULETTE

However beneficial government regulation may be in theory, there is no question that it has become expensive, burdensome, and often counterproductive in practice. Overregulation in the United States is deterring business start-ups and job creation, according to the international research consortium Global Entrepreneurship Monitor.[2] In 2004, the Small Business Administration reported that companies with fewer than 20 employees were paying over $7,600 per worker— 45 percent more than large corporations—just to comply with federal rules. A 2008 survey of 3,500 small firms by the National Federation of Independent Business (NFIB) found that "unreasonable government regulations" ranked among the top 10 problems cited by respondents. Each new federal rule, according to the NFIB, carries a price tag of $100 million in added compliance costs.[3]

New rules can also mean confusion and delay, as businesspeople file paperwork they don't understand and brace for changes they can't foresee. With no apparent rhyme or reason, responsible businesspeople are denied permits, turned down for public contracts, or fined for transgressions they never heard of. The unpredictability of the process has earned it the epithet "regulatory roulette."

Tales from the Dark Side: Disappearing Licenses

All-terrain vehicles in Oregon—often used in the state's agricultural and recreational industries—were licensed for years by the Department of Motor Vehicles (DMV). Then a change in state law transferred this responsibility to the Parks and Recreation Department. In the process of shifting bureaucratic oversight, someone in Parks decided that the DMV had lacked explicit legislative authority for the registration of ATVs for use on public roads.

In effect, long-extant ATV licenses disappeared. Overnight, law-abiding drivers became subject to tickets and fines. As one newspaper observed: "The impact was ridiculous. Suddenly a farmer or rancher doing his daily chores was . . . a criminal. The outcry was sharp, from the agriculture industry, ATV retailers and the media."

Legislators quickly introduced a new law to right the wrong—but not before disrupting the business of hundreds of Oregonians whose only mistake was to follow the rules.

No state-by-state compilation of regulatory costs exists, but a California study gives a sour taste of these local burdens. According to a report mandated by the legislature in 2006 (and perhaps fittingly, delayed for a year after its deadline), businesses in the Golden State must shoulder a leaden burden: $493 billion to comply with a still-growing list of rules and mandates. On average, this means $134,122 per California firm—a third of the state's gross product. "We understand that some regulation is needed to have a fair and balanced market, but there needs to be a reality check," commented the director of the state chapter of the NFIB.[4]

These well-documented problems beg an obvious question: Why don't officials just stop regulating? Even if Washington insists its agencies must keep up with changing national conditions, state and local governments could just call a halt to new rules.

Or could they?

SECTION 3: THE REASON FOR RULES

Imagine you encouraged an employee in your restaurant to get some formal training. When she enrolled in a course taught by a self-described "international chef," you agreed to pay half the cost. Unfortunately, the teacher's credentials turned out to be accurate but meaningless—she had once been an assistant cook in Canada—and the course was a waste. You want your money back. But in your state, there is no oversight of restaurant education, and thus no recourse.

After you complained to your state legislator, he proposed a new law. It would place all restaurant schools under the jurisdiction of county boards of education, and set curricular and instructional standards. It would also require these schools to offer a proficiency test.

After helping your representative build support among other restaurateurs who had been cheated by phony instructors, you were delighted to see his legislation pass by a wide margin.

Now you're getting calls from people who expect results from the new law. When will it take effect? Where can they get more information? Who will administer the proficiency test? That's when you realize that getting a new law on the books is only the first step in a complex policy-making process. Obviously, not all new laws are welcomed by the business community. But even those that are championed by business must be transformed from ideas into concrete prescriptions.

No one can be helped by the restaurant education law until it is implemented, and there are dozens of implementation issues. Here are just a few:

- County boards in your state are divided into two divisions: "vocational education" and "academic instruction." Culinary management courses could be categorized as either, or both. Which division would provide the best oversight?
- The law calls for "curricular and instructional standards." Who will take responsibility for developing these standards? How will they be vetted?
- Who will develop and administer the proficiency exam? What will it cost?
- A course can no longer be legally offered if it does not meet the new standards. But if a shady operator tries to get around the new law, what are the procedures for documenting and reporting her behavior?
- If state funds become available to subsidize restaurant schools, how should the monies be distributed?

These issues can only be resolved by new regulations pinpointing who will take charge of what, when each action will take place, and how it will be monitored. That means writing rules. So you find yourself eagerly anticipating these rules—the same rules everyone loves to hate.

Of course, there was a period in history when government acted without formal, written rules. The advantages were speed and efficiency: Citizens didn't need to wait for agencies to study, debate, and compose elaborate regulatory documents. But the disadvantages were weightier. With no firm guidelines, individual bureaucrats simply made their own decisions about how to administer the law—decisions that could be idiosyncratic and unfair. It was almost impossible to predict or challenge their judgments. Although some contemporary rule writers can be slow, obtuse, or overzealous, at least they improve the odds that government will treat everyone evenhandedly.

For better or worse, rules have become so fundamental that their absence or inadequacy can hamstring the delivery of public services. Businesses can end up in the unusual role of demanding regulation instead of battling it.

Tales from the Dark Side: What Is a Pedicab?

Dictionaries define "pedicab" as a small, three-wheeled vehicle with a seat, pedals, and handlebars in front—in other words, a combination rickshaw/bicycle. Whatever they are called, these little conveyances have proved highly popular on the streets of New York.

Because pedicab drivers and passengers can be injured seriously by speeding cars, the City Council enacted a safety law in 2007. It provided for a new pedicab license, which would require registration plates, seat belts, upgraded brakes, and other features. Rules were written and ready for implementation a few months later.

But pedicab owners sued to block the rules, claiming they made it too easy for novices to enter the business. Two years later, a judge decided in favor of the owners. Different rules would be needed.

But this time, officials did not act quickly. Without rules, the police could not enforce the pedicab safety law. After a driver was struck by a taxi and seriously injured, the Pedicab Owners Association pleaded for action: " 'It doesn't make any sense: if we're arguing over who gets registration plates, that doesn't change the law that you have to have seat belts,' said [the association's lawyer]. 'We begged the city, for the sake of safety, to please enforce these things before someone gets hurt.' "

The city's reply: Without procedures and guidelines—rules—there was nothing to enforce. " 'This is not a question of me initialing the bottom of a piece of paper, and tomorrow everyone's out there regulating,' said [the commissioner of consumer affairs]."[5]

In the meantime, the police decided to define pedicabs as bicycles. The bicycle safety laws, appropriate or not, at least had a rulebook.

Another unanticipated but increasingly common situation: A law gets proposed, then withdrawn, when someone realizes that the rules necessary to implement it would be impractical—or ridiculous.

Tales from the Dark Side: Wiping Out a Quandary

In 2008, Florida legislators gave preliminary approval to a bill that had the best of intentions: to ensure that public restrooms were clean and provided basic supplies. For instance, the law would have required hot water, soap, and enough toilet paper for patrons.[6]

But how much toilet paper is enough?[7] To enforce the law, would restaurant inspectors measure the thickness of rolls? Count individual sheets? Interview restroom users?

The bill was wiped out without further legislative action.

There are other, more specific reasons for certain types of rules. Procedural rules explain the internal structure and normal operations of a government agency, often including an organizational chart. For example, you might look to these rules to learn how to obtain records from the agency, and how to appeal its decisions.

Interpretive rules offer insight into the agency's understanding of the laws it administers. Let's say you must comply with a licensing requirement to provide two transcripts from your professional school, each signed by a different administrator. To you, this seems redundant. But the agency has a responsibility to confirm key information, and they interpret that duty as calling for a double-check of your records.

Interpretive rules most often cause problems when they are vague. For example, some permitting processes require the applicant to give notice to "interested parties." Unless the rule includes a clear definition of that term—or unless you request one—it can open the door to a host of legal challenges.

Legislative rules are used to implement laws; in fact, they have the force of law. These rules can establish standards and qualifications, impose penalties or sanctions, and change previous rules. When an agency promulgates, or publishes, legislative rules, it is making a promise to the public that it will enforce the law consistently, fairly, and transparently, according to those rules.

Under some circumstances—such as an imminent threat to public health or safety—government can implement so-called emergency rules. This could happen if, for example, a natural disaster wiped out a city's reservoir and necessitated the immediate imposition of water rationing.

Especially when they are feeling overregulated, citizens tend to think only of how they are targeted by rules. But rules constrain government, too: Literally, officials must act in accordance with rules that govern rules. Most importantly, rules cannot be devised in the proverbial "smoke-filled room." From Capitol Hill to town hall, government is required to give you opportunities to participate.

SECTION 4: YOUR SEAT AT THE TABLE

It would be hard to find a state legislator who ran for office because of a burning desire to invent regulations. Elected officials generally see themselves as idea advocates, not rule writers. But as government and society have become more complex, lawmakers increasingly lack the time, staff, and technical expertise (sometimes the patience) to turn their ideas into realities. That's why public agencies have evolved into stables of professional rule developers, interpreters, and enforcers. In other words, when it comes to regulation, bureaucrats are now the key players in state government.

But that doesn't mean you are shut out. Although bureaucrats do not face voters directly, they are accountable to elected legislators who do—the same legislators who control their budgets. At the top of key agencies are political appointees, representatives of high-profile politicians who can order personnel shake-ups if they get wind of citizen complaints. Even career functionaries with strong job protections have reason to pay attention to the public.

There's another reason to seek a seat at the regulatory table. Bureaucratic decision making is in theory a systematic, thorough analysis of all alternatives, but in practice it is "the science of muddling through"—the title of a classic article written in 1959 by the political scientist Charles Lindblom. Lindblom recognized that even if they tried, it was impossible for bureaucrats, on a daily basis, to obtain all relevant information and evaluate every implementation option. Taking the pedicab example, it might have made sense for city rule-writers to study how pedicabs are regulated in every other country around the world.

But they didn't. Instead, they sought ways to tweak or modify other vehicle safety policies already on the books—and presumably, already shown to be effective in protecting New Yorkers. Is this an ideal approach? Probably not, but it is low-risk and certainly faster than a worldwide analysis. In Lindblom's view, "muddling through" is adequately, if imperfectly, responsive to the needs of the public. Pedicabs are not bicycles, but bicycle regulation is at least a reasonable starting point.

What does this mean to you? It gives you power. Rule writers are not scientific investigators who will dig up every data point and weigh every theory before rendering a judgment. For the most part, they are influenced by whatever information and points of view are right in front of them. This is your opportunity—you can get your opinion included in that limited, extremely critical mix.

In the second section of this book, you will learn about tools and techniques that can maximize the effectiveness of your participation. For now, it's important to understand the basics of making it happen—which seats, at what tables, are open to you.

Based on the federal model, state agencies follow a step-by-step rule-making process. Although details differ from state to state, the general framework and goals stay the same.

The process begins when the agency informs the public of its intent to propose new rules (or modify existing ones). This can be done via its website, though notification by postal mail may be required for government officials and others who request it. Typically, this "first notice" will state exactly how, when and to whom people can submit comments, including information, suggestions, and protests. It may also offer a rationale for the new rules, similar to a cost-benefit analysis. This is your first chance to take part in the process: Ask if you can sign up to receive a regulatory notice by email, generated as soon as the agency begins to act in an area of concern to your business. (Even if this service is not offered routinely, it may be available on request.) Alternatively, you can monitor the agency's agenda online or by subscribing to its monthly or quarterly newsletter.

A fixed period for public comment is always offered, typically 30 to 60 days. A cynic might argue that this feedback is a waste of time, but it is not. By law, agencies must accept and consider all input received by the deadline—and it is not unusual for deadlines to get extended, once or several times. Also, comments become part of the rule-making "record" and can be checked by anyone. If there is proof that agency decision makers ignored the feedback, their new rules cannot take effect, or will be rescinded. So this is your second opportunity: Submit copious comments.

The third way to get heard is by attending a public hearing. An agency may choose to schedule one on its own initiative. But in many cases, hearings take place only because they are requested by citizens or by other state officials. (Note: Sometimes there must be a minimum number of requestors, within a specific time period, to force a public hearing. Although the number may be as few as 10, you will need to check this requirement if you are planning to make a hearing request.)

Finally, the agency publishes the rule in the form it intends to enforce. But even when rule-writers think the process is over, it really is not. The public can still protest to legislators, who have the power to challenge the agency's budget and other prerogatives. Political scientists call this type of advocacy "fire alarms."[8] More directly, citizens in many states have access to regulatory oversight committees, which review rules before, during, and/or after the rule-making process. Most committees are made up of legislators or other officials, but there are exceptions: For example, North Carolina appoints members of the public to a Rules Review Commission.

These oversight bodies do not always have the authority to veto or rescind rules. Their activities may be ad hoc and informal. But at a minimum, they can catch the attention of other interested parties, officials, and the media. Sometimes, heightened scrutiny is all it takes to convince an agency to rethink a controversial proposal.

Governors, too, can intervene in the rule-making process. In some states, new rules cannot take effect without gubernatorial approval; elsewhere, governors (or their staffs) routinely review existing rules as well as proposals.

Here is a summary of your opportunities to influence the low-profile but high-impact rule-making process:

#1: Ask to be notified when the agency starts to write rules that could affect you.

#2: Submit detailed feedback during the public comment period. Check the Appendix for models that can be adapted to either a written form or as oral testimony.

#3: Testify at a public hearing; if the agency does not schedule one, request it.

#4: If you are dissatisfied with the agency's decision, make your concerns known to any regulatory oversight committee, to your legislator, governor, or (optimally) to all of them.

Always keep in mind that your rule-making comments matter, and your voice will be heard. Although many rule writers are plodding and unimaginative, most try hard to be fair. In fact, there are times when the process works well enough to surprise its (plentiful) critics. For example, the Florida Department of Environmental Protection held a series of public hearings on its proposal to require property owners to install an expensive pollution-control device. They got an earful of complaints, but also plenty of practical suggestions. The result: Agency officials abandoned their original plan in favor of the cheapest alternative offered by members of the public. One local newspaper editorialized: "Clearly, the DEP didn't just sit at public hearings . . . with fingers in ears and minds made up. The bureaucracy was cumbersome as ever. . . . But at least this time [it]is lumbering toward the most common-sense solution."[9]

SECTION 5: DIAGNOSING A REGULATORY PROBLEM

Even when you have learned to take part in the rule-making process, just complaining will not be enough. You may be convinced that every government rule affecting your business is harmful and stupid—and you may be right. But rules must be changed one at a time. And the only effective approach is to address the flaws specific to each regulation and situation. You will get nowhere by tarring all regulations with the same brush.

If you can diagnose some common regulatory problems, you have taken the first step to curing them.

Obsolete Rules

Rules that were once timely but are now out of date are among the most widespread regulatory headaches. Over a decade ago, the National Association on Administrative Rules Review noted that more states have a process to critique proposed rules than to review those long on the books—so-called "immortal regulations." The magnitude of the problem is glaringly obvious in the experience of Michigan, a pioneer in rules review. In 1995, after the governor ordered the elimination of obsolete rules, 2,500 were wiped off the books.

Obsolescence can be triggered by a single word. Until 2005, New Jersey laws characterized developmentally disabled citizens as "idiots." But more often, it is caused by obvious changes in the economy or technology. In the twenty-first century, it is silly to require "carbon copies" of an application. Few states would even try to ban the sale of musical instruments on Sunday—a law that remained on the books in South Carolina until 2008.

A recent boom in home-based businesses has led to challenges of decades-old restrictions on how people can use their properties. For example, Nashville's planning code allows residents to work out of their homes—as long as they do not meet with customers. In Gilbert, Arizona, home entrepreneurs are free to do business, but cannot store work-related goods in a garage. Increasingly, such provisions are being deemed obsolete—or, at least, unhelpful in the face of current economic realities.

Rules Applied Inconsistently or Arbitrarily

Usually, this issue comes up because of imprecise wording in the regulation. For example, to get a waiver of your town's restrictions on building height, you might be told to document that you have considered "reasonable" alternatives. But what is "reasonable?" Doesn't it depend on your budget, the character of the neighborhood, and/or the intended use of the building?

Worse, some rules lack lacks any judgment standards. Here is an example from a 2006 report critical of the regulatory climate in Minnesota:

> If you want to legally hang signs or erect billboards in Minneapolis ... the ordinance does not delineate any criteria ... [so] any qualified applicant can be turned down for any reason or no reason at all. At the same time, the city's Zoning Inspector has unilaterally imposed competency testing on applicants. ... Applicants, however, have no idea what they must show to receive his blessing because the inspector does not maintain any written standards or guidelines.[10]

Sometimes an agency is so blatantly unfair as to raise suspicions of cronyism or corruption. In Arizona, the Pest Control Commission came under fire for allegedly driving its critics out of business. The board was also accused of making rules just to get around restrictions on its authority. In 2009, legislators finally quashed the controversy by dissolving the controversial group.

Rules with a Disproportionate Impact on Small Business

The problem of disproportionate regulatory impact is so serious and widespread that attempts to solve it have become part of the mission of the U.S. Small Business Administration (SBA). The SBA Office of Advocacy is spearheading a movement to extend regulatory flexibility to all 50 states. In the conclusion of the book, you'll find more details about this set of initiatives to cut financial and administrative burdens on small firms.

As part of its effort, the SBA tracks success stories: regulations that would have slammed small business, but were successfully redesigned without changing their original purpose. In 2005, for example, the Illinois Department of Public Health (DOH) proposed a rule requiring all fitness clubs to have a lifesaving device called an *AED* (automated external defibrillator). This was not a problem, as most facilities already owned one. However, another provision would have required an AED-trained employee to be on the premises whenever the club was open—despite the fact that AEDs come with self-activated voice-prompt instructions. The Department of Commerce and Economic Development (DCED) estimated that this would cost clubs at least $598 per week.

Thanks to a regulatory notice, owners of small fitness clubs jumped on the issue. Supported by small business advocates and the DCED, they won a major victory: DOH officials decided to exempt those facilities that would have been hardest hit. Others were allowed to meet the requirement simply by training one employee.[11]

Clearly, the Illinois experience shows that small businesspeople can speak with a big voice—as long as they are well-informed and motivated to act.

Rules with Unintended Consequences

Over time, even the most well-intentioned rules can come to wreak havoc.

In 1966, the federal government instituted a policy intended to preserve historic artifacts. Before any state construction project can qualify for a federal subsidy, it must undergo review by archeologists or other experts. The structures that can qualify for protection are as varied as churches, bridges, cemeteries—and sewers.

Although most Americans support the goal of historic preservation, few are aware of sewer travails like those in Des Moines. In 2009, this Iowa city attempted to modernize its century-old sewers by lining them with plastic, a process much cheaper than ripping up streets to build new lines. Contractors were eager to get started. But preservation officials argued that the project could harm the vaulted brick structures as well as nearby artifacts, like Indian burial grounds. Not only did they hold up the work—they raised the possibility of requiring Des Moines to construct a sewer visitor center, noting that Paris offers public tours of its underground system. The cost of such a tourist facility was estimated in the high six figures.

But Des Moines sewers carry different kinds of runoff than Parisian sewers, often contaminated with deadly bacteria and noxious gas. Moreover, the city's Public Works Director pointed out that earlier excavations on the same site had probably destroyed anything of historic significance. "The idea that we should protect cultural assets, to me, seems intuitive, but at what point is there some sense of reason to it?" [he] asked.[12]

In this case, reason got a boost when local legislators drafted laws to expedite historic reviews and find less costly, commonsense alternatives. But other regulations have unintended consequences that are thornier and harder to reverse.

For example, most bicycle retailers welcomed helmet laws for young bikers as a way to encourage safer fun (and sell helmets). But research shows that these laws have reduced youth cycling over time, not only hurting sales but possibly encouraging kids to take up more dangerous activities. Whether or not regulators are concerned about this data, it would not be easy to turn back the clock.[13]

Rules that Do Not Conform to Legislative Intent

When legislators pass a law, they have some policy goal in mind. Good or bad, there is always a purpose for the action, called "legislative intent."

Unfortunately, legislative intent sometimes gets lost in the regulatory process. More commonly, it is badly distorted. In the case of New Jersey's "One Gun a Month" law, legislative intent derailed so quickly that rule making was stopped in its tracks. In fact, it became necessary to write two more laws to fix implementation problems with the first.

By limiting handgun purchases to 1 every 30 days, the goal of the legislation was to deter illegal trafficking. But officials, alerted by the business community and lawful weapons owners, quickly realized the restrictions could drive gun shops out of the state. Licensed retailers could not buy in cost-effective quantities from registered wholesalers or manufacturers. Gun customers were barred from exchanging one product for another at the same store, unless they waited for a month.

Legislators solved these problems with a second law, explicitly exempting certain transactions—only to learn of still more market distortions. For instance, collectors were now prohibited from buying sets of historic firearms. Competitive shooters could not keep up with the needs of their sport. Yet another law was written to allow the state police to issue case-by-case exemptions.

The "One Gun a Month" law followed an unusually twisted path, but it finally arrived back at legislative intent. Things don't always work out that way.

Rules as Revenue-Generators

Regulation is not used just as a way to fill government coffers. At least it is not supposed to be. But sometimes, people wonder: As officials seek new sources of cash, are they turning regulators into bounty hunters?

In Newark, Delaware, an association of landlords fought rental permit fees 6 to 10 times higher than in comparable communities. Instead of offsetting the cost of inspections, opponents argued the cash was funding a general piggy bank for the town.

Similar allegations were made against the New York City Department of Health, after restaurant owners noted a 40 percent jump in fine revenues over three years. Inspectors claimed they were simply uncovering an increased number of violations, not deliberately chasing fines. But public opinion turned sharply against the sanitarians when they started ticketing street vendors for the way they stacked soda cans on food carts. The City Council forced the agency to back down.

When a group of California legislators interviewed 100 business owners who had left the state, they heard loud complaints about overly aggressive regulators. One small construction firm reported being inspected 150 times and assessed $9 million—in a year. " 'Government officials have basically become free enterprise entrepreneurs by creating profits from levying fines against businesses,' "[14] said one of the interviewers. This accusation may be overly broad— but it cannot be overlooked.

SECTION 6: HOMETOWN RULES

The administrative rule-making process is a creature of state government. But there are volumes of local rules, too, and a different avenue for influencing them.

In many policy areas critical to your business, town decision makers have little or no discretion. For example, they must enforce a standard minimum wage. Local health inspectors are required to check for violations defined by state statutes.

But in other matters, local government calls the shots. Even if higher-level officials disagree with municipal policy in these areas, they are powerless to change it. The procedures for licensing certain types of businesses, for example, are typically handed off to cities and towns—for better or worse.

Tales from the Dark Side: A Flowery Gamble

If you hope to sell flowers from a cart in certain cities, you must first win the lottery—literally. All applications for a flower vendor license, including renewals, are entered into a pool. The municipal licensing department draws names at random, assigning what it considers appropriate locations until they run out. Locations are not negotiable or transferable: any vendor unhappy with his spot is out of luck.

Towns are in charge of different matters in different states. Three common areas of local control include land use regulations, sign restrictions, and property maintenance codes.

Land use regulations define where businesses may locate and what type of structures they are allowed to build, rent, and occupy. Most often, "zoning rules" are used to delineate sections of the community as residential, commercial, retail, and industrial. But these regulations can reach much further. Especially in densely populated, highly developed municipalities, it is not unusual to find:

- Caps on the number of businesses of one type in the same neighborhood, like bars or parking garages
- Caps on the number of building occupants
- Restrictions on home-based businesses
- Landscaping and lighting standards, even for storage areas and parking lots
- Buffers for sensitive environmental features, like streams or steep slopes
- Restraints on building height, lot coverage, street frontage, and/or yard size

In many cities, every new structure must be approved by a design board. Its decisions can be the final word on architectural elements ranging from doors and windows to shingles and roof pitch.

There are procedures to appeal these decisions and request waivers of the rules, called "variances," but the processes are cumbersome and the outcome is never assured. Many an entrepreneur has hemorrhaged cash while awaiting a zoning decision that ultimately went against him.

It is not just the uncertainty of these decisions that frustrates variance seekers. Sometimes a zoning debate is not only prolonged, but picayune to the point of absurdity.

Tales from the Dark Side: Unfair to Chickens?

The concept of "accessory use" is routinely relied upon by zoning decision makers as a basis for granting, or denying, a variance. It means that the property owner engages in some activity not usually predominant on the site, but common and generally accepted by the community.

In Cambridge, Massachusetts, the definition of "accessory use" became highly contentious, involving charges of discrimination—against chickens. When a poultry owner argued for permission to house his birds behind his property, 90 neighbors showed up at a three-hour hearing to debate the role of chickens in cities.

The owner offered evidence that " 'henkeeping has a long history in urban settings,' citing that people all over the world have been keeping domestic ducks and chickens in urban areas for

---

thousands of years." Nonetheless, officials ruled that downtown chickens are no longer customary, meaning that—at least in Cambridge—a coop is not an acceptable accessory use.

At least one neighbor expressed disappointment, saying " 'I don't understand how chickens can be singled out and discriminated against because they are different.' "[15]

Sign restrictions can make or break mom-and-pop businesses, especially small retailers reliant on signage to lure shoppers away from the mall. Thanks to the First Amendment, towns cannot control what your sign says (unless it is fraudulent or slanderous); but they are routinely permitted to regulate its size, style, and overall visibility. Heavily residential municipalities may ban vivid colors, night lights, and three-dimensional protrusions. Even in commercial districts, there can be tight control of the number and proximity of signs; in thickly-signed tourist destinations, for instance, businesses often face new restrictions whenever someone complains about "sign pollution."

Property maintenance codes are the local rules imposed by town officials to uphold what they believe to be the standards of appearance and upkeep desired by the community. Some require only minor tasks like removing empty garbage cans from the street, or clearing snow from footpaths. But in their zest to prevent eyesores, the writers of maintenance rules can create major headaches, especially if the wording is vague or ambiguous. When is the paint on your storefront "faded"? This is a significant issue if you could be forced to repaint. Who determines if your landscaping is "neat"? That official could order you to uproot bushes. What, exactly, is "clutter"? When is a garden "overgrown"? For many small businesses, property maintenance codes are a source of ongoing frustration as well as unexpected costs.

So how can you have your say about local policies like land use regulations, sign restrictions, or property maintenance codes?

Unlike state agencies, local governments do not offer a distinct rule-making apparatus. In municipalities and counties, regulations are typically implemented by "ordinance"—the same type of local law applied to other municipal matters, ranging from tax rates to speed limits. This is a challenge, because every town has its own governance procedures. But it is also an opportunity. When you comment on a state rule, your opinion is one among many. When you take on a town regulation, you can be the star of the show. Moreover, ordinances must be voted up or down by political officials who are directly answerable to the voters.

In Section II, you will learn how to make the most of hearings, one-on-one meetings, and other avenues to influence local officials. But the best way to start is to recognize the far-reaching significance of decisions made in your backyard.

It is also helpful to keep in mind these key differences between state rule making and regulation by local ordinance:

- Local regulation is less orderly and predictable than the state rule-making process, but it is easier for an individual business owner to influence.
- Local ordinances are voted on by elected officials, while most state rule-making decisions are made by agency bureaucrats.
- Because they are generally more visible in the community, local ordinances are more likely than state rules to keep up with changing times.

On the other hand, there are important similarities:

- At both levels, regulations are more numerous and intrusive than ever. In the last decade, state rules reached into corners of the marketplace as obscure as the temperature of hot tubs and the texture of cooked eggs. There were local ordinances limiting the configuration of firewood piles and the use of perfume in public places.
- Regulation begets more regulation. For instance, when one occupational group is licensed and overseen by government, there are calls to extend similar oversight to others—with or without evidence that the extra scrutiny is needed.
- In both state rule making and regulation by local ordinance, there are multiple opportunities for input, and mechanisms to ensure the public is taken seriously.

KEY POINTS TO REMEMBER

- In the near future, regulation is likely to shift increasingly from Washington to state and local governments.
- The bureaucrats who write state regulations are not directly answerable to the public. But they cannot ignore the politicians— particularly legislators and the governor—who control their agencies' budgets.
- The ordinances that create local regulations are enacted by elected officials who want your vote.

- All regulations have their own flaws and problems. They may be equally bad, but for different reasons.
- You have many opportunities to influence the regulatory process, but it is up to you to take advantage of them.

NOTES

1. Quoted in L. Epstein, "Obama Opens the Door to More State Regulation of Business," *Daily Finance* May 22, 2009, www.dailyfinance.com.

2. S. Shane, "Time to Cut Red Tape for Startups," *Business Week* December 29, 2009, www.businessweek.com.

3. B. Phillips and H. Wade, "Small Business Problems and Priorities," NFIB report, 2009.

4. Quoted in J. Norman, "Jan Norman on Small Business," *Orange County Register* September 23, 2009, www.ocregister.com.

5. M. Grynbaum, "Pedicab Safety Rules Were Never Put Into Effect," *New York Times* June 12, 2009, www.nytimes.com.

6. "Toilet Paper Bill Moves Forward," WESH Orlando news report, March 22, (2007)

7. "Proposed Law Looks to Wipe Out Problem," cbs4.com news report, March 12, 2008.

8. M. McCubbins and T. Schwartz, "Congressional Oversight Overlooked: Police Patrols vs. Fire Alarms," *American Journal of Political Science* 28 (1984): 165–79.

9. Editorial "Bureaucratic Beast Plays Nice," *Palm Beach Post* January 11, 2009, www.palmbeachpost.com.

10. N. Dranias, "The Land of 10,000 Lakes Drowns Entrepreneurs in Regulations," report of the Institute for Justice, May 2006, p. 2.

11. State Guide to Regulatory Flexibility for Small Businesses SBA Office of Advocacy, 2007, www.sba.gov.

12. Quoted in J. Clayworth, *The Des Moines Register* July 27, 2009, www.desmoineregister.com.

13. C. Carpenter and M. Stehr, "Intended and Unintended Effects of Youth Bicycle Helmet Laws," *National Bureau of Economic Research Working Paper* January 2010,, www.nber.org.

14. Quoted in E. Zimmerman, "State Regulations Hurt Small Business," November 2, 2009, SanDiego.com.

15. X. Yu, "Chicken and Duck Owners in Cambridge Lose Appeal," *Harvard Crimson* February 12, 2010, www.thecrimson.com.

3

All Politics Is Local

OVERVIEW

If you tell your neighbor that you hate local politics, you are making a harmless observation. But if you don't pay attention to local politics, you are making a serious mistake.

Too many small businesspeople make that choice because they think of local politics as sleazy and inconsequential. The truth: Although it can be unsavory, you cannot afford to ignore it. The political world at every level tends to attract larger-than-life personalities who can be abrasive and confrontational. But whether or not local policy makers are likeable, on your home turf you have easy access and a direct line of communication to them. More to the point, you can position yourself to influence how they allocate government resources and power.

Section 1: What's at Stake I

How is local business affected by local politics? This section discusses some of the key impacts.

Section 2: The Most Important Politicians You've Never Heard Of

This section will teach you what you never learned in civics class: who wields the power in local elections, and what is the source of their influence.

Section 3: What's at Stake II

The prize in any political race is winning public office. Here you will find descriptions of the most common elective offices in different forms of local government.

Section 4: The Workings of a Local Political Campaign

In this section, you will learn why business input is highly valuable to a grassroots campaign.

Section 5: Getting Involved—Investors, Participants, and Civic Entrepreneurs

Political involvement can take many forms. This section describes the most common approaches.

Section 6: Danger Signs

Some candidates will not hesitate to act unethically—even illegally. To protect yourself, you must be alert to signs of trouble.

* * *

SECTION 1: WHAT'S AT STAKE I

The process labeled "local politics" actually has an impact well beyond a single locale. Although it does produce hometown leaders, it is also an incubator for politicians at higher levels. Aspiring state lawmakers, in particular, commonly begin as mayors or county commissioners. Many top state agency officials began their careers running municipal boards or departments.

Beyond its role as a springboard for future policymakers, local politics can have an outsize influence on the implementation of state and federal laws. For example, notwithstanding pressure (and grants) from Washington to spend on social services like mental health and drug abuse programs, local governments differ widely in how—or even if—they use the funds. One town might create a full-blown treatment center; another could choose to refer its needy residents elsewhere. What accounts for the differences? As one county-based study explained: "We find that local policy outputs are influenced by counties' ideological dispositions where more liberal/conservative counties produce more liberal/conservative outputs across a wide range of policy areas including public health, educational services, and welfare."[1] In other words, within the constraints of federal mandates, local officials are responsive to the political opinions of their constituents.

Many state laws are "permissive," meaning that it is up to local politicians to decide whether to enact them. Small businesses are extremely vulnerable when mayors or commissioners can choose whether to impose a fee, increase a tax, or enact a regulation.

For example, some states grant local governments the authority to slap builders with so-called "impact fees" on any new structure to defray the cost of roads, sewers, and other public improvements. These fees become particularly contentious during economic downturns, when towns are under pressure to expand infrastructure with shrinking budgets. Why are impact fees enacted regularly in parts of these states but never in others? Almost always, it comes down to the political visibility of local construction-related businesses. For instance, when the mayor argues that impact fees are the only source of funds for widening a bridge, builders can make the case that their projects will bring a new stream of tax revenues to replenish the town budget.

Virginia's battle over car taxes in the late 1990s showed how even a high-profile gubernatorial campaign can turn on local politics. Republican Jim Gilmore won the election by promising to roll back an unpopular assessment on cars and trucks. But the tax was not collected by the state; it was based on the value of personal property and levied by each local government at a different rate. Because residents of property-rich communities in Northern Virginia stood to gain far more from the rollback than other voters, the statewide contest became a regional tussle, pitting town against town. At the polls, tax foes in the North overwhelmed other voters, sweeping in a new governor— and years of ongoing local debate. Town-by-town implementation of the rollback became so controversial and unwieldy that Gilmore's plan was suspended with barely a whimper just a few years after it started with a bang.

But local politics would be important to small business even if its influence were confined to town hall. For better or worse, it is the system that gives rise to local regulation, taxation, and policy decisions that can be commerce-friendly—or hostile. Political allies of elected officials end up on zoning boards, redevelopment authorities, and other bodies with influence over your market opportunities and how you are allowed to pursue them. To a significant degree, the outcome of local political contests determines your quality of life—both personal and commercial.

Given this impact, why do so many businesspeople shun local politics? Of course, it involves some time commitment; but businesses routinely accommodate other activities, like philanthropy, that have less impact on the bottom line.

One reason is its shady, ugly image. Unfortunately, politicians have brought this problem on themselves. The real harm caused by public corruption (discussed in the next chapter) is compounded by perceptual damage done by the mudslinging and fear-mongering now routine in local campaigns. This is not to say that national races are free of acrimony—in fact, they have become increasingly bitter—but as one campaign expert points out: "I proposed a law of politics in the same vein of Parkinson's Law or Murphy's Law. My law read, 'The sleaziness in any political campaign is inversely proportional to the size of the election district.' "[2]

Make no mistake: The goal of a local campaign can be considerably less than high-minded. Some people run for office to avenge personal grievances or pay back petty slights. Others just want attention. A handful of politicians are overtly racist or xenophobic. It is these kinds of candidates who engender public wariness—if not outright disgust.

Voters understand that tight races often turn negative. They accept the legitimacy of criticizing an opponent for committing a crime, lying to the media, or otherwise behaving irresponsibly. But they are not eager to sniff dirty laundry for its own sake.

Tales from the Dark Side: What a Bum!

This excerpt from a campaign flyer in a 2007 legislative race speaks for itself: *[This candidate] Tried to Avoid Supporting His Own Child!*

In 2006, [this candidate] filed court documents pleading for relief from paying child support. [He] told the court he no longer had a source of income, as he had chosen to campaign full time rather than work.

> Why couldn't he contribute to his daughter's care? . . . So he could change careers and become a politician! If [this candidate] can turn his back on his own family to chase his ambitions, how can he represent yours?

The use of scare tactics is another visceral approach that alienates voters over the long term. Some local campaigns deliberately exploit people's anxieties about environmental hazards like pollution, high-risk facilities like jails and power plants, or pocketbook threats like new taxes. Sounding an alarm may be warranted in extreme circumstances: For instance, a candidate who learns of an imminent bridge collapse would be justified in trying to scare travelers away from the bridge. But these situations are rare. Politicians are on shaky ethical ground when they deliberately frighten voters, spread unreliable information, or pit one group against another.

Often this approach will backfire, as it did for a Republican candidate running in Nassau County, New York. Aware that voters were extremely worried about reassessment of their properties, she ran on a single-issue anti-reassessment platform. Her campaign materials promised a vigorous fight to stop "the Democrats' tax reassessment scheme."[3]

But the reassessment had been approved months earlier by a bipartisan majority of the county legislature. When this fact was publicized, the candidate was widely criticized for fear-mongering. She lost the election.

Fortunately, most people who choose to take on the hard work of politics are responsible, realistic, and motivated by some genuine policy interest. It may be issue-specific: For example, Jane may run to reduce a local tax. It may be process-oriented: John might seek faster disclosure of budget documents. Either way, candidates focused on improving government tend to see more success than those with little more than animus—if only because, in marketing terms, they can build more appealing "brand identities" in the political marketplace.

Another major reason why businesspeople steer clear of local politics: To any novice, no matter how successful in other fields, the political landscape can be as murky and mysterious as the Amazon. The process of selecting candidates, developing platforms, and running campaigns is fairly orderly, but it is guided by norms and customs that vary widely across states, counties, and towns. The unwritten rules are fully comprehended only by insiders who learned by doing, by accident, or by mistake. It can take hours of hunting, online or on the phone, to find even the most basic facts—who is who, what matters, where to get help.

The problem is not that information is deliberately hidden from newcomers. Although some insiders will not go out of their way to be helpful, most are eager to attract new blood. The stumbling block is what economists call "the curse of knowledge." People who have been part of a complex system for many years simply can't appreciate how confusing and intimidating it is to those who have not. As one writer put it: "Once you've become an expert in a particular subject, it's hard to imagine not knowing what you do. Your conversations with others in the field are peppered with catch phrases and jargon that are foreign to the uninitiated. When it's time to accomplish a task . . . those in the know get it done the way it has always been done, stifling innovation as they barrel along the well-worn path."[4]

In the face of so many disincentives, is it really worthwhile to get engaged with grassroots politics? What could you gain, for instance, by contributing time or money to a local campaign?

Section 5 will discuss some specific benefits. But as a general rule, you will find that the payoffs of this investment—in relationships, insight and access—are not only valuable, but unattainable in any other way. Some people mistakenly believe that by supporting a presidential candidate, for example, they will somehow win points with the town Democrats or county GOP. In fact—ideological parallels aside—local campaigns are, for all practical purposes, independent spheres of activity.

No roadmaps exist for the politically uninitiated. But there are landmarks: key players in the election process and basic features of a campaign.

SECTION 2: THE MOST IMPORTANT POLITICIANS YOU'VE NEVER HEARD OF

Political parties are the basic units of American democracy. In other countries, party money and power are concentrated at the national level. But the hearts of U.S. party organizations are their state and local participants. When it comes to electing candidates—the raison d'etre of any Democratic or Republican group—virtually all important decisions and activities bubble up from the grassroots.

A party is structured like a ladder. On the bottom rung are approximately 180,000 election precincts, each including up to a few hundred voters. Party members in each precinct (or group of precincts) elect representatives during primaries, who in turn choose party decision makers, called *committeepersons* on the next two rungs: the municipality and county. In most regions, county committees wield the lion's share of influence in local party affairs: endorsing candidates, raising money, and recruiting campaign workers. State and national party committees are higher up the ladder, but for the most part their role is to supplement, not supplant, the work of the counties.

So the members of a county committee are the most important politicians most people have never heard of. Few novices appreciate what they do, or how much they know. But it is not an exaggeration to say that the vast majority of America's elected officials owe their power to these low-profile volunteers.

The average county committeeperson has four main sources of influence. First, she is on a first-name basis with every official party leader and unofficial power broker. She knows who matters most in the local hierarchy, why, and to whom.

Second, she is likely to belong to other clubs and organizations. A national survey of local party leaders found majorities regularly engaged in community-building groups, events, and activities.[5] This means she is in a position to identify issues, make introductions, and forge alliances.

Third, county committee members are committed to the political process and aware of the importance of "retail," or grassroots, campaigns. Although media-driven and web-based races are increasingly widespread, street smarts will always matter on a local level.

Finally, in states where candidates are nominated or endorsed in party conventions, county committeepersons serve as delegates. The votes they cast can make or break the future of aspiring governors, U.S. senators, and even presidential contenders.

However, anyone on the front lines of a political battle is likely to take some bullets, mostly rhetorical but still hurtful. The role of the unpaid foot soldier is not only time-consuming, but often thankless and unpleasant. In recent years, both major parties have begun to have trouble recruiting and retaining county committeepersons. One measure of the problem: In a 2006 survey conducted in New Jersey by the nonpartisan Citizens' Campaign, 40 percent of the state's 24,554 committee seats were found to be vacant.[6]

Although state parties cannot pay committeepersons, there are movements afoot to give them more autonomy and responsibility. New Jersey's Party Democracy Act is one: This 2009 law expands the role of the county committee in selecting legislative candidates. Elsewhere, party organizations are mounting newly aggressive outreach and training programs. One way or another, the clout of these grass-roots activists is on the upswing. It is well worth cultivating and learning the ropes from them. You will find county committee members easily accessible: After all, they are your neighbors—and possibly your customers.

The local party chairman, selected by the committee, is often a forceful—some say domineering—presence. Many chairmen do not come up through the precinct ranks; often they are businesspeople with extensive political contacts. Their role is usually less potent in public than behind the scenes, where they spend enormous amounts of time raising money for campaigns and party-building efforts. At a minimum, chairmen can influence many other party players to support (or oppose) a candidacy. They are likely to be owed lots of favors, and unlikely to be shy about calling them in.

Most party chairman put in long hours for no more compensation than pride in a job well done. But others have been known to trade on their influence and connections for personal gain, brazenly and sometimes illegally.

Tales from the Dark Side: He Only Wanted to Help

In 2007, the political world of Brooklyn, New York, was riveted by the corruption trial of Democratic party ex-chairman Clarence Norman. Formerly one of the country's most entrenched power-brokers, Norman stood accused of extorting over $20,000 from an aspiring judicial candidate. Allegedly, he routinely helped himself to campaign funds, using them as rewards for his friends and cronies.

Norman was sentenced to 3 to 9 years in jail. But not before making a statement to the press: "The bottom line is I was convicted of asking candidates to pay their pro rata share of campaign expenses . . . That's it. That's why I stand convicted of a felony. For helping people."[7]

Since 2003, dozens of venal bosses (both Democrats and Republicans) have been prosecuted for egregious behaviors they once considered business as usual: bribery, extortion, bid-rigging, and tax fraud. On the heels of these scandals, legislators and courts, formerly loathe to intervene in partisan matters, have begun to step in. For example, a Michigan judge slapped down a power grab by party leaders in

2007: Their attempt to get exclusive access to voter lists would have strangled the campaign of any candidate who tried to run without their support.

Like New Jersey's Party Democracy Act, these initiatives represent progress but cannot root out every abuse. However, the combination of increased media scrutiny and emboldened critics is likely to succeed, over the long term, in replacing many of the local parties' remaining tyrants and crooks.

SECTION 3: WHAT'S AT STAKE II

The ultimate goal of a political party is power. Whether the power in play in a given election is that of a small-town mayor or a big-state governor, partisan loyalists pursue it vigorously and single-mindedly. They know that today's local official could be tomorrow's national leader. And in the short term, they also know the basic calculus of politics: to the winner go the spoils. In government, this means appointments, jobs, contracts, and influence.

However, different elective officials have widely varying types and degrees of power, even on the same governing body. To better understand the local political scene, it is helpful to be familiar with the basic structures and policymakers in local and state government.

Municipal Governments

Your municipality may be known as a town, city, township, village, or borough. Whatever the name, it is the level of government closest and most responsive to citizens—at least, to those citizens who learn the system.

A council (sometimes called a *board of aldermen*, *supervisors*, or *trustees*) is the legislative body of municipal government, where local ordinances and regulations originate. There can be as few as three councilpersons, or dozens. Some are elected to represent just one district, or ward; others are chosen "at large," meaning they are supposed to represent the entire population. Council elections are nonpartisan in over half of U.S. municipalities—but local political organizations often align with candidates despite the absence of party labels on the ballot. In partisan council elections, candidates are nominated by their party's town or county committee, or by winning a party primary.

A mayor is the most visible elected official in city hall. Most people assume he is also the most important. However, how much power he actually wields is entirely dependent on the form of government. There are four common forms: strong mayor-council, weak mayor-council, council-manager, and municipal commission. (Certain regions and rural areas have distinctive variations. In particular, New England towns elect administrative boards called "selectmen," and provide for citizens to exercise legislative power in periodic "town meetings.")

If Mayor Smith is elected in a strong mayor-council town, he is a chief executive officer with dominant administrative and policy-making authority. He appoints department heads and hires other key staff to advance his agenda, controls or heavily influences the budget, and can veto most actions of the council. Smith is probably a Democrat or Republican, though a strong mayor could be independent or nonpartisan.

Smith would experience culture shock if he moved to a weak mayor-council municipality. There, he could recommend policy to the council, but the members would have no obligation to listen. Important administrators, like the tax assessor and budget director, might be directly elected by the voters, meaning they would not owe Smith their jobs. To a significant degree, Smith would be able to act only at the pleasure of other officials—who may or may not belong to the same political party or share his ideology.

In a council-manager government, the mayor's job is largely ceremonial. Limited mostly to cutting ribbons, proclaiming holidays and the like, Smith would have far less authority than the city manager, a professional administrator. That official, accountable to the legislative body as a whole, would drive most day-to-day administrative, budgetary, personnel, and policy decisions.

Municipal commissions combine executive and legislative powers in one body. Each commissioner is chosen in a nonpartisan election to function as the head of one or more town departments or agencies. Collectively, with or without a mayor, the commissioners pass laws and set policy.

You will need to choose your approach to municipal government based on which of these forms it takes. Chapter Five will discuss your options.

County Governments

Counties may serve as few as 42 people (Loving County, Texas) or as many as 9.1 million (Los Angeles County, California). They may be compact and homogeneous, or sprawling and diverse. Some counties have responsibilities independent of other levels of government, and most levy their own property or sales tax. But their autonomy is limited: Counties exist largely for the purpose of allocating and coordinating state services among a designated group of cities and towns.

In most counties, a board of commissioners (often called *supervisors*) is elected to exercise both legislative and executive authority. A chair may be chosen either by the voters or by the commissioners themselves to run meetings and provide general oversight. Each commissioner takes responsibility for one or more areas of government, like land use planning, education, or transportation.

Certain functions are in the purview of other elected officials; for example, there may be a county sheriff to manage public safety, a prosecutor to enforce the law, a clerk to oversee records, and an assessor to administer the collection of taxes. In some regions, voters also elect a county executive to take on a mayor-like role. Typically, a professional county administrator is hired by the commission to fuse all these disparate pieces into a reasonably coherent whole.

The number of county chieftains can make for a fragmented, nebulous chain of command and a challenge for citizens who need to access the system. You will revisit this challenge in Chapter Five. To add to the confusion, multiple types of judges and magistrates are also elected to preside in county and local courts.

State Governments

Across the United States, state governments have a structure more consistent than counties or municipalities. Based on the federal model of separation of powers, there are distinct legislative, executive, and judicial branches designed to check and balance each other.

One or more state lawmakers, or legislators, are chosen in partisan elections to represent distinct, population-based legislative districts. They have the power to make laws and set policies. With the exception of Nebraska, all state legislatures are bicameral: This means citizens elect members of a lower house (generally called a *house of representatives, house of delegates,* or *general assembly*) and an upper house known as the *state senate.*

Many legislatures are part-time, convening to vote on bills for only a few months each year. However, the business of state government must move forward whether or not the legislators are in session. For this reason, professional legislative staff play a major role. They provide continuity, stability, and expertise to lawmakers, and a critical point of access to constituents.

In the majority of states, voters also elect state judges, including Supreme Court justices. State trial and appellate judges hear both civil and criminal cases. The Supreme Court has the power of judicial review, meaning that it can invalidate laws determined to be inconsistent with the state constitution.

Executive authority rests with the governor and other key officials, including the lieutenant governor, attorney general, treasurer, and auditor. State departments and agencies are in charge of specialized functions like housing, education, labor, and commerce. The governor and lieutenant governor may be the sole executives directly elected by voters; at the other extreme, almost every key agency head may appear on a statewide ballot. Either way, because of the size of the population they serve and the vast scope of their responsibilities, state executive officials are far less accessible than lawmakers. However, their departments maintain staff whose full-time jobs are to interact with the public. Like legislative staff, they offer wide-open doors onto the corridors of power.

This is the basic lay of the land from the perspective of a political activist, who might hope to snare one of the many public posts available in her state. In addition to elected offices and paid administrative jobs, there are also hundreds of spots on volunteer advisory boards and influential policymaking bodies. As a businessperson with market-tested skills and judgment, you, too, could pursue such an appointment. For example, almost every city has its own land use boards, economic development committees, tourism commissions, and other commerce-oriented citizen panels.

SECTION 4: THE WORKINGS OF A LOCAL POLITICAL CAMPAIGN

To the outside world, a campaign appears to hum smoothly like a well-oiled machine. But inside the headquarters (in a small-town race, this could mean the candidate's kitchen) it pulses wildly with frenetic, ever-changing activity. Before you consider getting involved in a local political campaign, you should be familiar with what makes it tick.

Whatever the office a candidate is seeking, he will have three primary needs: people, information, and money. And no matter how rich his campaign becomes in these resources, there is always room for more.

People

A political campaign is time-pressured, labor-intensive, and detail-oriented. In a hometown, low-budget contest, most of the work involves scheduling the candidate's time and coordinating volunteers and vendors. In a large-scale, media-driven campaign, there must be staff to manage cash flow, advertising, press relations, and field operations. Just as in running a business, technology has helped speed up the daily grind; but when it comes to making strategic decisions, there is still no substitute for talent and judgment.

What kinds of people add value to a campaign? First, most should be willing—indeed, eager—to help without pay. Media and supply costs will quickly drain the bank book of even a wealthy candidate, leaving little for salaries. But within the pool of volunteers, those with business experience are especially sought after.

Unskilled supporters are always welcome in a campaign; they can take on important nuts-and-bolts tasks like distributing flyers, making phone calls, and erecting lawn signs. But people with knowledge of marketing and management—like you—are worth their weight in gold. For example, perhaps you advertise your product on local radio. If so, you are in a position to recommend the best stations, a great help to a candidate with limited promotion funds. If you juggle schedules and delegate tasks among a dozen employees, you could readily manage campaign volunteers. Do you negotiate with vendors? That skill could bring down the cost of everything from paper to pizza.

Information

Every candidate needs a message. It is her brand identity—the way she positions herself in the marketplace of competing candidates. Ideally, the message will be positive, distinctive, and memorable. It should also be simple enough to boil down to one catchy sentence.

No one has yet invented a message template that can guarantee success. But experienced politicians know what doesn't work: an empty, vapid collection of words unconnected to local issues. To develop a message that will resonate with voters, all campaigns need solid information about community concerns.

But no candidate can be everywhere, know everyone, or be aware of every problem. Although polls can take the pulse of the public, they are unaffordable in many local races. So campaigns must rely on local supporters to be their eyes and ears in the neighborhoods.

One of the most valuable advisors to any local candidate is a businessperson willing to gather information from Main Street—even better, to translate that information into action, like writing a speech or arranging a public forum. Information from the small business community can stir important local debates: Do zoning rules stifle home-based entrepreneurs? Are city taxes hurting downtown stores? Effective advocacy can benefit businesses as much as it helps the candidate: The better he understands their issues, the more effectively he can articulate them during the race and, hopefully, address them after he wins public office.

Money

Political campaigns cost money, no matter how small the district or how frugal the candidate. Every voter outreach tool has a price: advertising, signs, flyers, phone banks. From clipboards to coffee cups, dozens of incidental expenses add up. A big city or countywide campaign can easily raise and spend more money in six months than a small business handles in a year.

Covering the costs herself is increasingly untenable for the average local candidate. Nor is the self-funding option necessarily desirable, as it fails to demonstrate community support. For better or worse, running for office means chasing donations. Every time someone comes through, even with a small amount, it counts as a step toward victory.

SECTION 5: GETTING INVOLVED: INVESTORS, PARTICIPANTS, AND CIVIC ENTREPRENEURS

If a well-meaning neighbor claims there is only one effective type of political involvement in your community, he is wrong. In every campaign, each approach has pros and cons. Here are the three major options:

Investor

A campaign investor simply writes a check. She does not take time away from her business or risk unpleasant confrontations with supporters of opposing candidates. In fact, a businessperson who can afford it will sometimes hedge her bets by investing in the campaigns of both sides.

Investor advantage:
- Donations in any amount will always be noticed and appreciated, even in a large-scale campaign.

Investor disadvantages:
- Every political donor becomes part of a mailing list used by other campaigns and partisan organizations.
- It is easy to run afoul of complicated campaign contribution laws.
- No matter how much you donate, a competitor could (and probably will) donate more.
- Under most circumstances, political donations are not tax-deductible.

Participants

Volunteering as an active campaign participant is, of course, more time-intensive than writing a check, but it is also more personal and distinctive. If you hope to be appointed to an advisory board, this is an excellent type of exposure.

Don't discount the fact that every political campaign is an exercise in marketing, management, and finance. Apart from these specific advantages, you can also gain general practice in high-stakes decision making.

Participant advantages:
- You can build lasting relationships with candidates and party activists.
- You may make useful contacts among other participants—officeholders, opinion leaders, and businesspeople.
- You will learn what gets the attention of politicians.
- You will have an opportunity to shape policy debates.
- By helping to elect a good candidate, you will help to improve government.

Participant disadvantages:
- You will make enemies among the political opposition.
- You could be identified as a partisan loyalist, even if you're not.
- To make your participation worthwhile, you will need to commit considerable time to the campaign—probably more than you expect.

Civic Entrepreneur

Civic entrepreneurs differ from traditional political activists. In fact, the term was coined not by political scientists but by economic development experts. Typically, these are local business leaders who recognize a need to foster collaborations with government. When civic entrepreneurs get involved in politics, their primary goal is to win support for ideas that will, in their view, expand markets, jobs, and public-private partnerships. In particular, they welcome innovation, creativity, and risk.

Civic entrepreneur advantages:
- By bringing your ideas to the table, you could drive a new public discourse.
- You could forge new alliances and identify common interests among disparate groups.
- If you wish, you could avoid being identified with a political party.

Civic entrepreneur disadvantage:
- Your sphere of influence would be limited to those candidates and activists who share your perspective and take an interest in your issues.

Politics is not for everyone. A meaningful commitment to a local campaign requires an intensity of focus and level of energy you may not be able to spare from your business. Also, political involvement can damage the reputation of certain professionals, like journalists, scholars, or public opinion pollsters, who are expected to be scrupulously nonpartisan.

If you are a high-profile decision maker for a hospital, foundation, university, or other nonprofit institution, your partisan alignment could compromise the legal or fundraising status of the organization. If you work in an industry like municipal finance or gambling, your state may prohibit a range of political activities. Although state and local public employees are generally free to engage in campaigns (federal workers must comply with special restrictions), they cannot use government resources or do any political work on government time.

Other reasons to steer clear: You are engaged in litigation with a public body (in this case, ask your attorney). You fear publicity. Other businesspeople in your community have reported bad experiences with local politics. Or you simply find it distasteful.

There are plenty of legitimate concerns. But now you have enough knowledge of the system to make an informed judgment about what is right for you. If you decide to stay away from local politics, at least make a commitment to stay alert—to the issues, the players, and their potential impact on your business.

SECTION 6: DANGER SIGNS

For as long as there have been political campaigns, there have been unethical candidates. In fact, ethicists observe that "In practice, political campaigns represent one of the circumstances most likely to bring out the worst in people. Many candidates seem to subscribe to the theory that almost anything is allowable in order to get elected, because once in office, they will be outstanding public servants."[8]

So you must protect yourself. As a general rule, you should always say no to a politician who makes you uneasy or a tactic that seems unsavory. More specifically, watch out for candidates who:

Put the Squeeze on You

If a candidate pressures you to hire one of his friends or steer business to his donors—don't. The kind of candidate who takes advantage of his supporters will make the kind of public official who looks out for his cronies instead of his constituents.

The same goes for a candidate who threatens some kind of retribution, perhaps a boycott of your business, if you fail to donate. Ninety-nine percent of the time, her threat will be empty—but if something actually comes of it, you can respond by calling the press, the police or the opposing candidate.

Make Light of, or Ask You to Circumvent Campaign Finance Laws

Every state has its own raft of restrictions on how and in what amounts you may donate. This category of laws, known as "pay-to-play," is designed to stop politicians from giving public jobs or contracts in return for contributions; the problem is discussed in Chapter 4. But there are many other rules with equally important purposes. For example, to foster transparency, campaigns can be required to disclose the names and occupations of every contributor on a state database. This allows citizens, journalists, and other candidates to track who gets support from which interests.

Remember: In campaign finance law, "Everybody does it" or "No one cares" are not acceptable excuses. What seems a minor violation can be a serious offense, and donors may be as culpable as candidates. In general, alarm bells should ring anytime you are strong-armed to donate in cash, or to inappropriately alter a check.

Expect You to Enable Dirty Tricks

Publicly, no one endorses campaign tactics based on deception or misrepresentation. There is no guide to political dirty tricks. But behind closed doors, some candidates argue that the end (winning the election) justifies the means (dubious activities). They make a deliberate decision to jettison truthfulness and fairness.

Do not enable them. If they tell you that their tactics are legal, they may be right: political advertising, for example, can make representations and promises that would never pass muster in ads for cereal or soap. But legal or not, shady tactics corrode the electoral process and undermine the public's faith in local politics.

The techniques devised by the political underworld are limited only by their imaginations (and budgets). Here are two of the more common types that you could be asked to fund or facilitate:

1. Push polls

    A political poll is a legitimate research tool. A push poll is a fraudulent form of telemarketing, designed to dish dirt on a candidate under the guise of research.

    Unlike genuine voter surveys, push polls are typically very short (only one or two questions) and extremely negative toward a candidate or issue. The caller avoids naming the source of the call and will not explain how the information is being used or by whom. She asks questions like these: Would you vote for Betty Smith if you knew she abandoned her illegitimate child? Do you support Tom White even though he has been accused of extortion?

    Even when there is a shred of truth to such slurs, the push poll is a deliberate attempt to distort and sensationalize them. For instance, Tom White may indeed have been accused of lawbreaking. But the criminal complaint could have been filed by his opponent, based on fabricated evidence. Bottom line: If a candidate tells you he needs a donation to pay for a poll, make sure it is a real one.

2. Cyber-deception

    Technology has enabled a new generation of tricksters. Do not allow your computers (or your funds) to be used for online shenanigans. These might include campaign emails disguised to look like they originated from a government office or a nonpartisan group; "phishing" messages that furtively obtain voters' personal data; and anonymous or fake-name blog posts.

Tales from the Dark Side: A Phony Fan

When a San Francisco blogger named Rita posted unflattering photos of Mayor Gavin Newsom, she drew a response from someone identified as "John Nelson:" " 'This Rita chick is kind of weird with her angry infatuation. . . . Get over it sister, he is a good mayor.' "

"Nelson" was found to have written from the home computer of Gavin's press secretary and political booster. It was not an isolated incident: Members of the Board of Supervisors called for the spokesman to be fired after learning that he " . . . apparently has been using phony names to post comments on popular blogs . . . building up the mayor and blasting his critics and reporters."[9]

Encourage You to Lie or Coerce Others

You could be asked to recruit supporters under false pretenses, lie to vendors, make dubious statements to the press, or coerce others to do so. Just say no.

Have a Bad Reputation

If a candidate has a good name in the community, it speaks well of his ethics. The opposite is also true: a candidate with a rascal's reputation probably has earned it.

KEY POINTS TO REMEMBER

- Hometown politics has far-reaching effects.
- The lion's share of power in local elections is wielded by grassroots activists—your neighbors and customers.
- Getting involved in local politics can yield benefits—relationships, insight, and access—that are otherwise unattainable.
- Different types of involvement each have their own strengths and weaknesses.

NOTES

1. G. Percival, M. Johnson, and M. Neiman, "Representation and Local Policy: Relating County-Level Public Opinion to Policy Outputs," *Political Research Quarterly* 62, no. 1 (2009), 20.
2. L. Grey, *How to Win a Local Election* (M. Evans: New York, 1999), p. 208.

3. M. Cooper, "In Nassau County, a Small Election Will Settle the Political Balance," *New York Times*, May 1, 2000, www.nytimes.com.

4. J. Rae-Dupree, "Innovative Minds Don't Think Alike," *New York Times*, December 30, 2007, Week in Review Section 3, www.nytimes.com.

5. P. Bearse, *We, the People* (Lafayette, LA: Alpha Publishers, 2004).

6. D. Walsh, "A Political Army in Need of a Few Good Soldiers," *Star Ledger*, April 9, 2006, www.starledger.com.

7. A. Ginsberg, "3-Time Loser Norman Guilty," *New York Post*, February 24, 2007, www.nypost.com.

8. J. Nadler and M. Schulman, "Campaign Ethics," Markkula Center for Applied Ethics at Santa Clara University, 2006, www.scu.edu/ethics.

9. D. Noyes, "S.F. Mayor's Aide Accused of Dirty Tricks," KGO-TV/DT January 30, 2007, abc7news.com.

4

The Corruption Tax

OVERVIEW

You've never greased a palm, paid a bribe, or forked over a kickback. But public corruption still robs you—and your customers—both of money and of trust in government. Honest businesspeople rely on an honest marketplace, and cannot compete when officials deal with crooks. Citizens are hurt when shoddy work slips by in return for payoffs. Communities suffer when public jobs are steered to unqualified cronies, undermining quality of life and discouraging private investment.

To ensure a free, fair, and healthy local market, it is essential to be educated and vigilant about the major types of public corruption—and the dubious behaviors that can nurture and camouflage it.

Section 1: The Roots of Corruption

Corruption has no single cause. Instead, dubious behaviors are rooted in—and abetted by—long-established structural and political forces.

Section 2: The Corruption Tax

It will never be labeled on your tax bill, but you pay a considerable price for corruption wherever and whenever it occurs.

Section 3: Slippery Slopes

Certain dubious behaviors, when rationalized, excused, or overlooked, are often the first step down a path of iniquity.

Section 4: A Rogue's Gallery

This section highlights a few particularly notorious crimes of local corruption and the shameless former officials who wreaked havoc by committing them.

* * *

SECTION 1: THE ROOTS OF CORRUPTION

Few state or local governments are actually rife with corruption. But there are enough to create an impression of nationwide perfidy. Even as you read this book, hundreds of mayors, commissioners, legislators, and other government officials will be starting their terms—in jail. Between 2006 and 2008, the FBI convicted over 18,000 officeholders who bribed, cheated, extorted, and stole from the public.[1]

Compared to the hundreds of thousands of honest officials, this sordid group is small. But it doesn't take a dragnet to undermine public confidence, especially in a local community. In a small town, even a single indictment looms large. The downfall of one trusted leader, like a judge or sheriff, is enough to sap civic pride. At a time when every errant politician attracts around-the-clock media attention and blogosphere buzz, it is all too easy to believe that crooks run amok throughout government. In 2005, nearly 90 percent of those polled by the Associated Press described public corruption as a serious problem.[2] Two years later, only 10 percent of respondents to a Pew survey believed the country was "making progress" against corruption, while almost half said it was getting worse.[3] The public's cynicism feeds on itself: As one political scientist describes this phenomenon:

> Revelations of scandal, or the belief that wrongdoing is common even if it never comes to light, can upset one's general image of the way politics works, or who wins and loses and how, and of one's own ability to influence government. While idealized pictures of American politics have never fully corresponded with reality, they can still be matters of great emotional investment. This is not to say that everyone starts out with these ideals in mind, only to suffer some loss of political innocence later. But for those who hold at least a few of these perceptions, corruption can strike a heavy blow.[4]

What causes the slide of powerful people into ignominy? Reacting to a spate of corruption in 2006, a *New York Times* analyst observed: "Arrogance gave way to recklessness, which in turn opened the door to criminality."[5] Tellingly, however, this observation was not about government: It described Enron, the business behemoth that collapsed in iniquity. Clearly, the hubris that poisoned corporate culture can seep into the public sector too.

More specifically, there are deep-rooted structural and political forces helping to breed corruption. Chief among them is the extreme fragmentation of government. As mentioned in Chapter One, states can be carved into thousands of jurisdictions, each with its own governing body and taxing authority—and minimal if any oversight. In practice, this means that legions of officials have unchecked access to billions in public funds. Politicians in some states routinely hold multiple government jobs, creating public fiefdoms where no one dares to question the boss. When so many individuals have an independent power base funded on the taxpayer's dime, the odds are overwhelming that a few will give in to avarice.

Some scholars tie recent upswings in corruption to increasingly intrusive government regulation. Every new rule, they argue, creates an opportunity for officials to bend or break it in return for payoffs. As the bureaucracy grows, so does the number of potential thieves. "If you want to cut corruption cut government," advises economist Gary Becker.[6]

Many parts of the country have weak or nonexistent ethics laws, and lax enforcement is often a problem even where rules are tough. Many towns—even entire states—are Wild Wests of ethically questionable but technically legal behavior. For example, an official may give government jobs and contracts to members of his family, accept valuable gifts from government vendors, and continue to serve in public office even after being indicted for corruption in that office.

Where it is allowed, the practice known as "double dipping"— holding more than one public position simultaneously—is particularly corrosive. In New Jersey, some local officials have held over a dozen posts each. The problem occurs because the holder is obligated to serve different masters, all with their own, often conflicting, interests. Amid the tangle of responsibilities and expectations, the official often ends up serving no one but herself.

Tales from the Dark Side: Everybody Does It

Before being convicted of bribery and fraud, former New Jersey state senator Wayne Bryant was one of the most powerful members of the legislature, routinely steering millions in public funds to favored individuals and institutions. In return, he allegedly received at least one no-show job to pad his taxpayer-paid pension—on top of three other government positions.

His defense? " 'You may not like it,' [Bryant's attorney] Carl Poplar said of the multiple job holdings, 'but it's not illegal and it's not uncommon.' "[7]

Another factor: the complexity and cost of today's local government. In early America, even the greediest official had little to steal. Public institutions were scarce and expenditures were modest. But today's venal small-town mayor—let alone a big-city alderman or state lawmaker—has access to millions in cash and public property. As expenditures continue to mushroom, on everything from parcels of land to management consultants, so do enticements to thievery. Some unscrupulous operator is always ready to offer a five-figure bribe in return for a seven-figure government contract. It can also be tempting to "borrow" cars, computers, or other public resources.

When a jaded public gives up on honest government, the result is a lack of interest and involvement in local elections, as evidenced by low voter turnouts. Despite hot contests for several city commission seats in Florida's chicanery-riddled Broward County, for example, over 90 percent of voters in the 2010 election stayed home. No one doubted the reason. Noting the "languid spell" cast over the local races, a journalist observed: "The few voters who showed up to cast a ballot attributed the pervasive voter apathy to recent reports of government corruption in South Florida." One resident commented simply: "People have lost interest. . . . [They] are fed up with corruption in local government."[8]

Public scrutiny deters abuses of power. Conversely, officials are more likely to cut ethical corners when no one is looking. Unfortunately, there is a vicious cycle: When corruption causes citizens to turn away from government, their inattention encourages more corruption.

Procedural transparency, too, is inimical to thievery. But government spending practices can be murky and misleading. The best known of these questionable methods is "earmarking," used by members of Congress to direct taxpayer money to pet projects without debates or votes. Earmarking came under heavy fire after former Representative Duke Cunningham went to jail for taking bribes in return for these appropriations, but legislators debated for years before restricting the popular and long-entrenched practice.

Similar types of under-the-radar discretionary spending are available to officials in some cities and states. Members of the New York

City Council, for example, quietly showered millions on favored organizations and institutions—until the public learned that members routinely allocated funds to phony groups, with names like "Coalition of Informed Individuals." The fakery was a convenient way to disguise the magnitude and purpose of the actual disbursements.[9] State legislators may insert so-called "member items" in their budgets, the practical equivalent of earmarks. Among the local projects funded without debate in the 2008 to 2009 Texas budget were a zoo, a soccer complex, and a skate park.[10]

Finally, politicians can make matters worse by looking the other way. Notwithstanding recent rock stars of public corruption like former Illinois Governor Rod Blagojevich—indicted for allegedly trying to sell a U.S. Senate seat—most offenders are low-level, small-time crooks. Even when they are not, it is easier to dismiss them as aberrations than to acknowledge the flaws in a system that facilitated their crimes. For instance, after Connecticut Governor John Rowland pleaded guilty to mail and tax fraud, ending months of scandal that tarnished local officials around his state, House Speaker John Amann allowed that government was "wounded." But he was also quick to repeat what can become a mantra in political circles: "Most people [in government] have their hearts in the right place—to serve the public."[11]

Amann's point is well taken. But when lawmakers disregard corruption, they miss an opportunity to head off future misdeeds—and bolster public confidence—with stronger laws, training, and oversight.

Corruption has many faces. Here are three major variations:

1. Bribery: An official is paid, usually in cash, to deliver a vote, job, or other official action. For example, former Governor Rowland steered business to government contractors in return for free renovations of his summer cottage.
2. Extortion: The converse of bribery, extortion is the threat to withhold an official action unless the extorter is paid. A health inspector might threaten to report code violations unless a salon owner produces a "gratuity."
3. Discrimination in administration of law or application of the rules: Common examples are ticket-fixing or granting a license without documentation, usually in return for some kickback or favor. Federal investigators caught 26 employees of the Arizona Department of Motor Vehicles issuing fake driver's licenses and identity cards.[12]

SECTION 2: THE CORRUPTION TAX

There is no such thing as "trivial" public corruption. Whatever its form and scope, it is a serious drain on the economy wherever and whenever it occurs. As mentioned in the previous section, communities pay an indirect price in political and civic disengagement. More directly, businesses and residents shoulder a hefty "corruption tax."

The corruption tax is "levied' in at least four ways.

1. Overpriced, Shoddy Goods and Services

When government contracts are awarded to businesses in return for bribes or kickbacks, not only are honest competitors shut out, but expenses are typically padded to cover the illicit payouts. Moreover, a company that gets contracts through crooked deal-making has little incentive to deliver quality service—or any service. A federal investigation into Chicago's "Hired Truck" program, for example, found that firms bribed officials in return for hauling contracts but actually performed little or no work.[13]

2. Wasteful Expenditures

Corrupt officials look for opportunities to create no-show jobs, give out unnecessary or overpriced contracts, and hike public salaries to reward their allies in government. They rarely hesitate to incur public costs for private benefit. For instance, former Pennsylvania legislator Mike Veon allegedly used state employees to drive two motorcycles to South Dakota so the bikes would be ready when he and his wife flew there for a vacation.[14]

3. Damage to Economic Vitality

Corruption may drive existing businesses out of a community, leaving a bigger tax burden on those who remain. Political arm-twisting can discourage firms from bidding on public contracts or developing expertise in serving local needs. Even a whiff of official impropriety can be a deal-breaker for companies looking for a place to locate or expand. As summarized by one economic development expert: "There is an issue with trust in the political system, being able to rely on a certain set of rules. . . . Corruption creates tremendous uncertainty, and uncertainty is bad for business."[15] According to the U.S. Attorney for Eastern Louisiana—who indicted 213 state and local officials and their private accomplices over seven years—rampant corruption in New Orleans had facilitated a "brain drain" and a decline in the city population, to 450,000 from over 600,000, long before Hurricane Katrina.[16]

4. Costs of Investigation and Prosecution

It is not unusual for a high-profile corruption case to drag on for a decade or more, with taxpayers footing the bill. For example, the investigation of former Illinois Governor George Ryan—eventually convicted for fraud and racketeering—took 13 years. Such pursuits are not only expensive; they suck up other legal and judicial resources already insufficient to fight violent crime and social ills.

Although the corruption tax cannot be quantified with precision, estimates are eye-popping. At the federal level, the General Accountability Office has calculated that the amount siphoned off by theft and fraud is at least 10 percent of expenditures on all federal government programs—tens of billions of dollars.[17] In Chicago, the cost of corruption has been pegged at around $300 million.[18] In New Jersey, an estimated price tag of $1 billion has never been documented but is considered realistic. "It's not that a billion dollars in cash actually changes hands each year," says a former head of the Prudential Business Ethics Center at Rutgers University. "But if you believe that corruption distorts incentives so the right decisions are not being made, then a large number like that makes sense."[19]

SECTION 3: SLIPPERY SLOPES

Few government officials are born crooks. They do not enter public service eager to abuse the people's trust.

But in the course of doing their jobs, many officials find themselves at the edge of a slippery slope: an ethically ambiguous or challenging decision point. Taking a dishonest turn at that juncture leads to increasingly dubious behaviors. Say a building inspector spots a defect in a structure being sold by his friend, a local developer. If he reports the violation, it will kill the sale. So he deliberately overlooks it, justifying the decision to himself as a harmless, one-time favor.

The problem is that one favor facilitates another. Deceit is like any other learned behavior: The inspector finds it easier every time he does it. As he develops a reputation for being "helpful," he is sought out by favor-seekers. It is only a matter of time until he is offered cash in return for coming through. In fact, an extensive federal bribery probe of Chicago's Building and Zoning Departments snared dozens of just such "helpful" officials. Over more than a decade, these investigators falsified reports, altered computer data, and coached developers in how to circumvent city codes. In return, they received envelopes stuffed with money—in amounts pegged to the seriousness of the violations they had agreed to overlook.[20]

Of course, whether or not an official starts to slip toward iniquity depends on many factors, not least her own moral compass. Honest decision making is more than just obeying the law: Even the strongest code of ethics regulations cannot anticipate every choice between right and wrong. Being ethical means doing what is in sync with one's own values and standards, and with the expectations of the community. It also means striving to avoid harm to others, defined narrowly (family and friends) or broadly (the citizens). Two prominent ethicists describe ethics in public life as "not about selfishness, greed, scumbags; not merely compliance to the law; not finger-pointing . . . [but about making] difficult choices that create positive precedents and outcomes, and perhaps, even, make this a better place to live in."[21]

However, there are certain pernicious influences in public life with the potential to push a morally unsteady official over the edge. Among the most widely recognized are conflicts of interest, gifts, nepotism and cronyism, political patronage, and campaign contributions.

Conflicts of Interest

An official has a conflict of interest whenever his loyalties are divided: In other words, he has a personal stake in a public decision. Casting a vote can make him rich. Supporting a project can win him a job. Approving a contract can reward a political ally—or punish a foe. These situations crop up regularly in local government, where many decision makers serve only part-time and earn a living in the private sector. They naturally have business contacts, relationships, and investments that do not always line up with the public interest. For instance, Mayor Jones has a conflict of interest if his auto dealership seeks to supply the town's police cars. Board of Education Chairman Smith has a conflict if he owns land that the school district is considering for purchase.

Conflicts of interest are also the most common type of ethical dilemma faced by state lawmakers. According to the National Conference of State Legislatures, "Conflicts of interest typically arise when a legislator or staff member has the potential to receive a personal benefit based on his or her public position. Often, the personal benefit is a financial one."[22]

Money need not change hands to create a conflict of interest. Consider these scenarios:

- A State Supreme Court Justice intervenes with the prosecutor, police, and court officials to influence a case involving his son.

In each interaction, the justice goes out of his way to make sure he is recognized, pointedly handing out business cards to anyone who does not know his title.

- A city council staff member pressures a valet parking attendant to take responsibility for damage to his car. No proof exists that the attendant caused the damage. When the parking firm's managers appear, the staffer warns them that their permits "have to come through my desk in my office."
- Legislators with control of a university's state funding are treated to special tickets for its most sought-after football games. The tickets are largely unavailable to ordinary fans. They are also distributed to the mayor and many other local government officials—including the county engineer responsible for constructing and maintaining roads in the vicinity of the stadium.

Each of these examples is real. In the first situation, the New Jersey judge was censured for "misusing his office to advance a personal interest."[23] In the second, the Boston City Council staff member was fined $1,000; the Massachusetts ethics commission commented: "Using one's official position to influence the resolution of a private dispute can only undermine confidence in government."[24] In the case of the Ohio State University football tickets, no action was taken: The practice was questioned by government watchdog groups but defended by the college—and by the lucky recipients. (However, one lawmaker was forced to resign his seat after revelations that he sold his tickets on eBay for $13,000.)[25]

Some political scientists argue that divided loyalties are inevitable in citizen legislatures. They believe the cure—limiting lawmaking bodies at every level to full-time career politicians—would be worse than the disease. They may be right. But theories aside, there is no question that conflicts of interest can lead to duplicity, secrecy, double-dealing—or worse.

Tales from the Dark Side: Political Horse-Trading

For 14 years, Joseph Bruno ruled New York's State Senate with an iron hand. As Senate Majority Leader, he wielded near-dictatorial control over the distribution of state funds and the direction of critical votes.

But in December 2009, a 13-year federal corruption probe into Bruno's activities ended with his conviction by a jury. Reports of the trial summarized his crimes: "Bruno deprived the public of 'honest services' by using his position as one of New York's most powerful leaders to reap $3.2 million in consulting fees and by failing to disclose his conflicts of interest."[26]

In particular, prosecutors homed in on his relationship with an entrepreneur, Jared Abbruzzese, whose ventures received hundreds of thousands of dollars in state grants—after payoffs to Bruno. Jurors convicted Mr. Bruno of pocketing $200,000 in return for delivering the grants. In addition, "They also convicted him on one count involving a horse-breeding partnership that Mr. Bruno and Mr. Abbruzzese dissolved in 2005, with Mr. Abbruzzese forgiving Mr. Bruno $40,000 in debt and paying him $40,000 for a horse that prosecutors said was virtually worthless."[27]

Gifts

Few businesspeople would look askance at a box of candy from an employee, a bouquet of flowers from a customer, or a bottle of wine from a vendor. In the private sector, such tokens of appreciation are routine, even expected as a matter of courtesy. Why, then, should anyone think that a mayor can be bought for a lunch?

The problem is not the free sandwich. It is, again, the slippery slope. A suspicious, cynical public has reason to worry that today's innocent trinket can pave the way for tomorrow's bribe. For a crook, it is only a small step from accepting trifles to demanding tributes. Even an honest official can be tempted to twist arms, however gently, to help someone who has showered him with presents. Unfortunately, a trivial exchange can morph into an extravaganza of avarice.

Tales from the Dark Side: Selling Out for an Xbox

Baltimore, Maryland, saw a flurry of downtown building during the last decade. There was plenty of money to be made, and no shortage of developers eager to cash in.

For then-Mayor Sheila Dixon, there was also a chance to live the high life. According to state prosecutors, one prominent developer treated her to a mink coat, a Persian lamb jacket, costly beauty products, and lavish trips. She shook down another for gift cards, claiming they would be distributed to needy families.

Instead, Dixon used Best Buy gift cards to buy herself CDs, DVDs, a camcorder, a PlayStation 2, and an Xbox. She also stole Toys R Us gift cards intended for poor children.

A grand jury indicted Dixon on 12 counts involving theft, fraud, perjury, and official misconduct. Upon her conviction for embezzling the $500 gift cards, one juror commented: "The denomination doesn't matter. It's a trust issue."[28]

Nepotism and Cronyism

What is wrong with an alderman steering a contract to his old college chum? Why is Mayor Smith on a slippery slope if she hires her brother, an experienced lawyer, to represent the town?

Public officials who defend nepotism (preference for relatives) and cronyism (preference for friends) typically assert that these practices do no harm. In fact, they claim, taxpayers get better service from people with a personal motive to make government leaders look good.

Sometimes, that can be true. But it is beside the point. The presence of nepotism and cronyism means the absence of standards and safeguards. When these practices run rampant, there are no objective measures of performance. Private relationships take priority over public needs.

Worse, any type of favoritism creates a cynical workplace culture with no incentive for ordinary employees to improve. "Occasionally it was a joke when we saw a job announcement come out and we would say, 'I wonder who they want promoted now?' " said a worker at California's nepotism-riddled Unemployment Insurance Appeals Board.[29]

More broadly, nepotism and cronyism fly in the face of two bedrock American values: fairness and equal opportunity. Both are central to integrity, and the perception of integrity in government. As stated in New York City's public procurement rules:

> The underlying purposes of these Rules . . . are to ensure the fair and equitable treatment of all persons; to ensure appropriate public access; and to foster equal employment opportunities. . . . To this end, public employees and elected officials having responsibility for contracting at all levels shall encourage competition, prevent favoritism, and obtain the best value in the interest of the City and the taxpayers.[30]

Some argue that occasional favoritism is acceptable, even desirable. For instance, why not hire a councilman's uncle to work for the town if he happens to be available sooner than other applicants? But occasional impartiality is not a mark of good government—it is just another slippery slope. At any given time, an unscrupulous official can find staggering numbers of employable relatives and friends. When a manager for the Los Angeles Housing Authority steered contracts worth half a million dollars to his brothers,[31] for instance, it was hard to believe that no other firms were ready to handle the work. There can be no guarantee that merit will count unless it is built into basic hiring and purchasing rules, like these:

- Requiring competitive bids for products and services.
- Publicly advertising jobs and hiring criteria.
- Requiring officials to recuse themselves from votes that could benefit a relative.
- Documenting reasons for and against hiring and procurement decisions.
- Authorizing regular, independent audits of hiring and procurement decisions.
- Making audits readily accessible to the public.

Nepotism and cronyism are corrosive even when public expenditures are not involved. In an increasingly common twist, unethical public officials look to take care of their friends not with government paychecks, but by pressuring private employers to hire them. This can be justifiable if the official knows a job applicant and has a legitimate basis for recommending him. Some codes of ethics explicitly permit it: for example, New Jersey allows legislators to help a job seeker as long as:

> no fee, reward, employment, offer of employment or other thing of value is promised to, given to or accepted by the member [of the legislature] . . . and the member does not endeavor to use his official position to improperly influence any determination.

But what is "improper influence"? Is it writing a reference on official letterhead, thus suggesting that the applicant has some government imprimatur? What if the official calls a potential employer of her sister, subtly mentioning city contracts that could materialize in return for "help"? Clearly, it is at least a nascent form of corruption when a public office becomes a recommendation mill.

Tales from the Dark Side: The Friends and Family Plan

In 2002, officials in Miami-Dade County, Florida, faced a vexing problem. The rapidly growing, increasingly traffic-congested metropolitan area was in dire need of mass transportation upgrades that the government could not afford.

In pursuit of a new revenue source, then-Mayor Alex Penelas embarked on an ambitious campaign to win public approval for a half-cent sales tax dedicated to mass transit. It would not be an easy sell—voters had repeatedly rejected tax proposals in the past. But Penelas got high-powered help from the Transport Workers Union, whose members advocated enthusiastically for the so-called People's Transportation Plan.

The transit tax passed in November 2002. But it did not usher in the promised golden era of cutting-edge transportation for all. Instead, the tax proceeds fueled a hiring spree for a favored few: relatives, friends, and supporters of Penelas; various county commissioners; top county staff; and other local officials. Many of the hires were made indirectly, through a murky arrangement with temporary personnel agencies that discouraged public scrutiny. Background checks were skipped or ignored: At least four of the well-connected new employees turned out to have shady pasts or criminal records. During an earlier corruption scandal, one had taken over $50,000 in kickbacks.

To make matters worse, the managers also cut a backroom deal with the Transport Workers Union, never disclosed to the public or submitted to commissioners for a vote. The agreement reclassified hundreds of jobs so as to speed promotions and deliver big raises—less than a week after the 2002 election.

Over the next six years, details of what was dubbed the "Friends and Family Plan" leaked out as it became apparent that mass transit improvements would fall far short of Penelas' promise. The transit agency's payroll budget ballooned—there were 1,400 new employees, and the number of six-figure salaries more than tripled. But in 2008, Miami Metrorail had fewer trains than in 2002. Bus routes were cut back, and there was not enough money to replace aging vehicles.[32]

As one rider lamented, "We had temporary 24-hour bus routes. They disappeared. We had a temporary increase in bus routes. Most of them are cut. But I've seen plenty of people with jobs. They took care of themselves."[33]

Political Patronage

The practice of rewarding partisan loyalists with jobs or contracts is seen as a means of party-building—at least among those who believe that political support is for sale. This slippery slope is, however, on the decline in most of the country.

In the pre–World War II heyday of patronage, the financial muscle of party machines in New York, Chicago, Baltimore, and other large cities enabled them to bankroll virtually all local campaigns. When machine-backed candidates won public office, they paid their debt to the party by hiring the rank and file—and by turning a blind eye to bribery, racketeering, embezzlement, and myriad other forms of corruption.

But in the mid-twentieth century, civil service reforms made it difficult to continue rewarding party adherents with government jobs. Also, the spread of mass media and of modern campaign techniques freed candidates from dependence on the machines. In 1990, the U.S. Supreme Court delivered a further blow to what was left of the patronage system: In the landmark case known as *Rutan v. Republican Party of Illinois*, the justices declared unconstitutional "promotion, transfer, recall, and hiring decisions based on party affiliation and support," declaring them "an impermissible infringement on public employees' First Amendment rights."[34] (The Court recognized, however, that partisan loyalty may be relevant to some jobs, and that political affiliation may be taken into account if it serves the public interest.)

Where patronage lives on, it is now balanced by at least some degree of merit-based decision making. Although party machines still exist, they are held in check by legal scrutiny, public suspicion—and a new generation of civic activists for whom politics is its own reward.

Campaign Contributions

The cost of a modern political campaign would shock the candidates of yesteryear, who could not have imagined spending hundreds of thousands, even millions of dollars, to run for a state or federal office—and only marginally less to be competitive in a major city or county election. One reason is that contests at every level are increasingly media-driven; another is a steady drop-off in volunteers, forcing candidates to hire staff. The burgeoning industry called "political consulting" has created demand for pricey, high-tech services like micro-targeting research.

Whatever the causes, today's campaigns are akin to military arms races, focused on the acquisition of ever-bigger and more powerful weaponry. But unlike the army, candidates cannot stockpile arms unless they succeed in amassing private donations.

Like any other torrent of cash, political fundraising creates temptations to steal, hide, or divert resources; or, more specifically, to sell promises of action or access. There have been enough abuses to erode public trust in the integrity of the electoral process. In states with an elected judiciary, outsize donations to judicial candidates create the impression that verdicts are for sale. In response, every level of government now regulates how, from whom, and in what amounts politicians are allowed to raise money. With variations from state to state, there are caps, disclosure requirements, timing restrictions, and other rules.

Unfortunately, not even the strictest campaign finance regulations have come close to eliminating "pay to play": trading votes, jobs, or contracts in return for donations. These agreements are illegal, but prosecutors rarely succeed in proving a quid pro quo. So the practice is widely acknowledged to exist around the country as a system of informal, wink-and-nod exchanges, undocumented and readily camouflaged.

Pay-to-play exists in near-infinite variety. Some schemes are fairly primitive: for example, the former sheriff of Buncombe County, North Carolina, was convicted of extorting cash from video poker companies in return for allowing them to operate illegally. According to the indictment, he kept some of the money in the trunk of a car to keep it handy for his own gambling habit.[35]

At the other extreme of sophistication: As of March 2010, the U.S. Department of Justice was pursuing a multistate investigation into investment decisions involving hundreds of millions of dollars in public pension funds. If officials were influenced by political payoffs, as alleged, the crime would affect huge numbers of government retirees in California, New York, and New Mexico. In the New Mexico case, the state pension fund lost $90 million after investing with a firm run by large contributors to Governor Bill Richardson. According to a whistleblower lawsuit filed against the firm, "The defendants sold the state of New Mexico a worthless combination of liars' loans, lethal leverage and toxic waste. The pressure to invest in [the firm] was motivated by illegal and improper inducements—kickbacks or bribes in the form of campaign contributions."[36]

Tales from the Dark Side: "A Political Crime Spree"

Generally acknowledged as the poster child for pay-to-play abuse, former Illinois Governor Rod Blagojevich was taped by federal prosecutors as he engaged in what they termed a "political crime spree." The most sensational allegation: he schemed to auction the U.S. Senate seat vacated by President Obama to the highest bidder.

But prosecutors also argued that Blagojevich was a master influence-peddler long before he had a federal office to sell. Over eight years in office, he amassed $58 million largely from "favor seekers rewarded with state contracts, appointments and regulatory breaks."[37] In one instance, his price was $100,000 to sign legislation favorable to the horse-racing industry. In another, he sought $50,000 in return for a state allocation to Chicago's Children's Memorial Hospital. And $650,000 appeared to buy an appointment to the Illinois Gaming Board.[38]

As the *Washington Post* commented: "It's easy to look at Mr. Blagojevich's downfall . . . and ask: What's the matter with Illinois? But it's not just Illinois. The seamy story should prompt a reexamination at every level of government about whether enough has been done to preclude similar scandals."[39]

Of course, some government employees rob, cheat, and lie to the public just because they can—like the Illinois treasury official who opened a bank account under a false name in order to steal $250,000 from the state budget.[40] But there are bad actors in every sphere of human activity. While they can never be eliminated, they can be isolated—and caught.

SECTION 4: THE ROGUES' GALLERY

Public corruption is never a victimless crime. Sometimes, its impact is strong enough to permanently alter a municipality, county, or state. Those who commit such community-wrenching crimes deserve special dishonor. Here are three notable rogues:

Rogue #1: Marlboro, New Jersey, Mayor Matt Scannapieco

In 1990, Marlboro was a quiet rural community of 20,000, with a farming heritage and an all-American image. Fifteen years later, the population had doubled and every public facility was bursting at the seams. Local taxes had skyrocketed as the government struggled to cope with sprawl, congestion, environmental degradation, and over-crowded schools. Worse, Marlboro had become synonymous with corruption.

The man at the center of the town's transformation served as mayor from 1992 to 2003. He was an inveterate, gregarious booster of his community—especially among developers eying its hundreds of acres of open land. One of Scannapieco's priorities was to pack influential land use boards with his supporters—who made sure his developer friends got a royal welcome when they proposed projects that were oversized, overpriced, and under-scrutinized.

By 1997, the mayor was cashing in on these friendships. He inter-vened directly to get approvals for at least a half dozen high-cost, high-profit subdivisions, often at higher densities than normally allowed. In return, he pocketed $245,000. His allies were busy working their own big-builder relationships: A planning board member took bribes for pushing to rezone a 150-acre property, while the chairman of a municipal utilities authority engaged in extortion and tax evasion. Thanks in large part to the officials' foul play, 3,388 new homes were built in the 33-square-mile town between 1995 and 2005, far more than anyone had ever anticipated or prepared for.

Eventually the FBI was tipped off about the ring of crooked developers and the officials who did their bidding for a decade. When Scannapieco and his cronies pled guilty in 2005, it put an end to their crimes—but not to Marlboro's problems. As the new mayor, Robert Kleinberg, bitterly observed: "We're going to be paying for the corrupt acts of the former offi-cials for a long time to come ... [their convictions do not] unbuild the homes, uncrowd the schools or decongest the roads."[41]

In an unprecedented attempt to recoup some of the town's resources, Kleinberg filed suit against Scannapieco and his accompli-ces under the Racketeer Influenced and Corrupt Organizations Act. But RICO was designed to fight organized crime, not corrupt politi-cians; the case was dismissed in 2008. A judge ruled that Marlboro had no proof of specific, quantifiable injury—only a defrauded citi-zenry, a depleted budget, and a ruined reputation.

Rogue #2: Birmingham, Alabama, Mayor Larry Langford

After its steel industry collapsed in the 1970s, Birmingham clawed its way back to economic vitality. By the late 1990s, it hummed with growth and optimism. As the county seat of booming Jefferson County, Birmingham had become a regional center for banking, health care, and higher education. No one imagined that just a few years later, the county would be in such dire fiscal peril that it would be forced to contemplate asking the court for protection from creditors—in other words, filing for bankruptcy.

At the center of the collapse was Mayor Larry Langford, a colorful politician who never hesitated to think big. During his years in various local offices, he pushed to construct an amusement park, a domed football stadium, a trolley network, a Pentagon-style municipal building, and a canal to bring cruise ships into Birmingham—from 250 miles away. In 2008, he proposed a bid to host the 2020 Olympics.

But behind the scenes, Langford's real priority was sewers; more precisely, the complex financing deals undertaken by Jefferson County to pay off $3.2 billion in debt. The county had borrowed heavily— many said irresponsibly—for a massive sewer project with costs that spiraled out of control and sparked a host of shady borrowing schemes. Among the wheeler-dealers were two of Langford's friends, a local banker and a lobbyist.

The three conspired to pay the mayor hundreds of thousands of dollars, in cash and other valuables, for his help in steering county bond business to favored firms. The booty included a Rolex watch, designer clothes, audio equipment, and a $50,000 personal loan— arranged for Langford by his banker friend and paid off for him when he defaulted. For their part, his partners raked in hefty fees and payoffs. Meanwhile, Jefferson County descended into fiscal chaos.

But Langford's flamboyant behavior attracted suspicion. In 2007, he was investigated by the Securities and Exchange Commission, which ultimately sued him for taking $156,000 in bribes. In 2008, he and his accomplices were arrested by the FBI on over a hundred charges of bribery, conspiracy, fraud, money laundering, and tax evasion. Convicted in 2009 on 60 counts, Langford was sentenced to 15 years in jail and fined over $100,000. His cronies also received lengthy prison sentences. As the *Birmingham News* editorialized: "No wonder Jefferson County and Alabama are sick to their stomachs about corruption in government."[42]

But Langford's conviction did not end the financial debacle that he helped to create. Jefferson County still faces the possibility of bankruptcy—which, if filed, will bring about the largest municipal collapse in American history. One analyst put it bluntly: "Jefferson County is the scariest situation in the market today."[43]

Rogue #3: Massachusetts State Senator Dianne Wilkerson

In the late 1970s, a wave of public corruption in Massachusetts led to the formation of the Ward Commission, charged to find reasons for the breakdown and make recommendations for reform. Its final report concluded: "We have learned that corruption is a way of life in Massachusetts." Published in 1980, the Ward findings prompted a wave of ethics laws that went further than most supporters had hoped and were hailed as some of the best in the country.

Apparently, however, the early reformers did not anticipate all the modern opportunities for perfidy. Nearly three decades later, there was a new generation of scoundrels at the statehouse. A standout among them was Senator Dianne Wilkerson, chair of the powerful Joint Committee on State Administration and Regulatory Oversight.

A high-profile though controversial fixture on the Boston scene, Wilkerson was the first African-American woman to win a seat in the Massachusetts Senate. There had been previous run-ins with the law—she was convicted of failing to file federal tax returns and fined for violating state campaign finance and disclosure regulations. But until the very end, the loyalty of her constituents remained unshaken. Endorsed by the political establishment and buoyed by her prowess at the polls, she apparently felt unassailable. By 2007, she was actively welcoming the attentions of unscrupulous favor-seekers.

In an 18-month investigation, undercover FBI agents posing as businessmen caught Wilkerson taking bribes—up to $10,000 at a time—in return for development permits, liquor licenses, and legislation. Some of the more lurid exchanges were recorded on surveillance videotapes; one showed Wilkerson stuffing $100 bills into her undergarments. Here are a few highlights:

> A meeting at posh [Boston restaurant] No. 9 Park, where Wilkerson allegedly tucked 10 $100 bills into her bra; a two-day gambling spree at Foxwoods Casino after allegedly accepting a $1000 kickback at [a local cafe]. . . . At one point, she allegedly laughed after an undercover agent posing as a developer handed her $10,000 and said, "That's a lot of money." She boasted that she was "arm-twisting" and "knee-cracking" city and state officials.[44]

Inadvertently, Wilkerson rendered a public service. After being indicted on more than 30 counts of bribery and corruption—despite her claim that she had received only tokens of appreciation from grateful constituents—she became a symbol of all the shortcomings in state ethics laws that had been ignored since the Ward Commission.

Governor Deval Patrick formed a 12-member task force to recommend changes, but lawmakers continued to resist reform. Ultimately, Patrick threatened to veto a sales tax increase sought by the legislature unless it was accompanied by tightened ethics regulation.

In July 2009, Patrick signed an ethics bill hailed as "the most significant reform in a generation."[45] Among other changes, it doubled the penalties for bribery and banned legislators from accepting valuable gifts—provisions that will be remembered as legacies of Dianne Wilkerson.

KEY POINTS TO REMEMBER

- Although the vast majority of public officials are honest, all are tarnished by the corrupt acts of a few.
- Whatever its form and scope, public corruption always drains the local economy and penalizes honest businesses.
- Several deep-seated structural and political forces facilitate, even encourage, unethical behaviors.
- Conflicts of interest, gifts, nepotism, cronyism, and pay-to-play are among the most pernicious influences in public life.
- Ethics laws and policies cannot stop but can deter corruption.
- Ongoing vigilance is the best—indeed, the only—antidote to corruption.

NOTES

1. FBI Report, "Fraud and Corruption: Stemming the Surge," 2008, fbi.gov/fraud_corruption.

2. Associated Press, "AP Poll: Lawmaker Standing Falls," December 8, 2005, MSNBC.msn.com.

3. C. Cillizza, "Parsing the Polls: How Much Does Corruption Count?," April 17, 2007, Washingtonpost.com.

4. M. Johnston, "Right and Wrong in American Politics: Popular Conceptions of Corruption," in *Political Corruption: A Handbook*, edited by A. Heidenheimer, M. Johnston, and V. LeVine, 745 (Transaction Publishers: New Brunswick, 1986).

5. K. Eichenwald, "Verdict on an Era," *New York Times*, May 26, 2006, pp. C1, 6.

6. G. Becker and G. N. Becker, *The Economics of Life* (New York: McGraw Hill, 1997).

7. Quoted in C. Rothman, "Once-powerful Lawmaker's Corruption Trial Begins," *Star Ledger*, September 16, 2008, www.starledger.com.

8. J. Gollan, "Shechter, Castillo Keep Seats in Pines," *Sunsentinel*, March 10, 2010, www.sunsentinel.com.

9. R. Rivera and R. Buettner, "Speaker Says Council Allotted Millions to Fake Groups and Spent It Elsewhere," *New York Times*, April 4, 2008, p. C9.

10. A. Castro, "Much of Pork Spending in State Budget Going to Craddick Supporters," June 9, 2007, www.lubockonline.com.

11. House Speaker J. Amann, as quoted in L. Baldor, "U.S. Targets Government Corruption," *Boston Globe*, December 25, 2004, www.boston .com.

12. D. O'Brien, "Cracking Down on Public Corruption," Federal Bureau of Investigation Headline Archives, June 20, 2005, www.fbi.gov.

13. A. Zelinski, "Crooked Politicians Costing Illinois $300M in 'Corruption Tax': Professor," *Huffington Post*, March 30, 2009, www.huffingtonpost.com.

14. S. Duclos, "12 Pennsylvania Democrats Indicted in 'BonusGate,' " *Digital Journal*, July 11, 2008, www.digitaljournal.com.

15. T. Bartnik, as quoted in M. Hughlett and W. Wong, "The Cost of Corruption: Image of Dishonesty Can Hurt a State's Economic Vitality," *Chicago Tribune*, December 14, 2008, www.chicagotribune.com.

16. Quoted in N. Carey, "Fighting Corruption Is Hard Going in New Orleans," *Boston Globe*, August 14, 2008, www.boston.com.

17. O'Brien, "Cracking Down on Public Corruption."

18. Zelinski, "Crooked Politicians Costing Illinois $300M in 'Corruption Tax': Professor."

19. Quoted in M. Daks, "Cost of Corruption: $1B," *NJBIZ*, August 3, 2009, www.njbiz.com.

20. J. Coen, "Chicago Zoning Inspector Pleads Guilty to Taking Bribes," *Tribune Business News*, November 3, 2009, www.chicago.tribune.com.

21. E. Freeman and P. Werhane, presentation to the Emerging Leaders Program of the State Legislative Leaders Foundation, Darden School of Business, University of Virginia, 2007,

22. National Conference of State Legislatures website, "Conflicts of Interest," www.ncsl.org.

23. C. Toutant, "N.J. Ethics Panel Finds Judge Abused Office by Interceding in Son's Dispute, Urges Censure," *New Jersey Law Journal*, July 13, 2007, www.law.com.

24. M. Finucane, "Council Aide Fined in Ethics Case," *Boston Globe*, August 19, 2008, p. B3.

25. "I-Team: OSU Football—Who Gets Special Prices?," November 7, 2008, KYPost.com.

26. G. Blain, "Former State Senate Majority Leader Joseph Bruno Convicted on Corruption Charges Spanning 13 Years," *New York Daily News*, December 7, 2009, www.nydailynews.com.

27. N. Confessore and D. Hakim, "Bruno, Former State Leader, Guilty of Corruption," *New York Times*, December 8, 2009, www.nytimes.com.

28. J. Bykowicz and A. Linskey, "Baltimore Mayor Convicted of One Count of Fraud," *Baltimore Sun*, December 2, 2009, www.baltimoresun.com.

29. As quoted in J. Ortiz, "State Worker: Nepotism Poisons the Workplace," *Sacramento Bee*, November 27, 2008, www.sacramentobee.com.

30. New York City Procurement Policy Board Rules, Section 1-03, www.nyc.gov.

31. K. Roderick, "Corruption in the Housing Authority," *Los Angeles Times*, July 29, 2007, www.laobserved.com.

32. L. Lebowitz, "Transit Hires Included the Well-Connected," *Miami Herald*, December 21, 2008, www.miamiherald.com.

33. L. Lebowitz and R. Barry, "Gravy Train," *Miami Herald*, December 21, 2008, www.miamiherald.com.

34. *Rudan v. Republican Party of Illinois* (1990), 497U.S.62, p. 497.

35. Associated Press report on WTVD-TV Raleigh-Durham, "Jury Convicts Ex-Sheriff in Gambling Case," May 15, 2008, WTVD-TV Raleigh-Durham.

36. Quoted in M. Braun, "Pay-to-Play Cost New Mexico $90 Million, Lawsuit Says," *Bloomberg Press*, January 20, 2007, www.bloomberg.com.

37. Editorial, "Governor Blagojevich's Bombast," *New York Times*, December 28, 2008, Week in Review, p. 7.

38. C. Maag, "Illinois Impeachment Panel Hears of Fund-Raising," *New York Times*, December 23, 2008, p. A14.

39. Editorial, "Lead Us Not . . ." *Washington Post*, December 13, 2008, www.washingtonpost.com.

40. Zelinski, "Crooked Politicians Costing Illinois $300M in 'Corruption Tax': Professor."

41. Quoted in R. Smothers, "Officials Pleaded Guilty, But Town Was Changed Forever," *New York Times*, July 11, 2005, wwwnytimes.com.

42. Editorial, *Birmingham News*, December 4, 2008, www.bhamnews.com.

43. Quoted in B. Burnsed, "Bond Debacle Sinks Jefferson County," *Business Week*, November 8, 2009, www.businessweek.com.

44. M. Levenson, J. Saltzman, "Bribery Defendant Senator Wilkerson Allegedly Took Cash for Help in Liquor License, Development," Boston Globe, Oct. 29, 2008, p. A1.

45. Editorial, "A Season of Reform," *Boston Globe*, June 26, 2009, www.boston.com.

Part II

What You Need to Do

5

Get Smart I: Basic Research

No matter how smart you are in business, the skills don't translate: You must put in some effort to make yourself smart about government. Can you afford to spend time on research? Look at it this way: If you don't, expect to spend still more time making frustrating, fruitless mistakes.

Think of research as more than a way to educate yourself; it is also an advocacy tool. The most important key to influencing government is to give the right information to the right people at the right time. In fact, the majority of wrong-headed government decisions are made not because the decision makers are obtuse or ill-intentioned, but simply because the only data available to them when they need it is insufficient or incorrect. The ability to correct those inaccuracies and offer facts will put you in a position of power.

Every businessperson can become proficient at getting at least the basic facts about government. If you are still unsure why you should spend time doing research, here is another perspective:

> The essential purpose ... is to provide information which will facilitate the identification of an opportunity or problem situation and to assist managers in arriving at the best possible decisions when such situations are encountered.[1]

Note: This is the definition of *marketing research* from a classic business textbook. But the goal of government research is no different. Armed with information, you can identify opportunities, diagnose problems, and facilitate good decisions. More generally, you will be recognized as a knowledgeable, formidable advocate.

Section 1: Where to Look

This is an introduction to the major resources available to anyone with a computer—and a commitment to getting smart about government.

Section 2: How and When to Look

You will not get the right answers by asking the wrong questions. This section explains five procedural and timing guidelines.

Section 3: Getting Specific

Certain facts about government should always be at your fingertips. Here you will learn about specific types of information that can be useful over time and in a variety of situations.

* * *

SECTION 1: WHERE TO LOOK

You won't be surprised to learn that official government websites are the best places to start your research. What you may not expect: These sites have important limitations, especially if you are focused on a county or municipality. To maximize your efficiency (and minimize your frustration) it is helpful to understand upfront what these sites can deliver—and what they cannot.

As a general rule, state websites provide considerably more information, in more sophisticated formats, than local sites. Although there is no standardization among states—in fact, sites differ greatly in ease of navigation and degree of interactivity—in most cases, you can easily find overviews of each branch of state government (executive, legislative, and judicial); descriptions of state agencies (functions, services, processes, and leadership); listings of key regulations pertaining to in-state businesses; identification of business taxes, fees, and other financial obligations imposed by the state; voting and election rules; and links to major business resources and support services, such as employment training and loan programs.

Tips and Techniques

Unless you have a lot of experience navigating your state's website, chances are you will be stumped by some of its more arcane links or headings. Do not waste time clicking and scrolling through material that is far afield of your needs; instead, go directly to the home page search engine. Every state government is complicated both in structure and in terminology, and you might be pleasantly surprised when the information you want pops up somewhere you didn't know to look.

Few county or municipal websites can rival the online resources provided by a state. However, the smaller scale of local sites can allow for significant depth of information and a high degree of interactivity. For example, the zoning code of a town is often available online in its entirety, complete with downloadable maps, photos, and illustrations. With increasing frequency, local sites are making it possible to complete forms, file applications, and pay fees online. If you are marketing a product to the government, look for e-bids. You may be able to send questions not just indirectly (to a general email box) but also directly to the mayor and each department head.

Watch out for a key pitfall of local websites: information may be labeled in such a way as to obscure its source or purpose. From a practical perspective, this means you can't be certain what you are looking at. A link to "small business resources" could lump together both public and private programs. A budget line item called "general operations" could camouflage a slush fund. If there is no clear definition, request one.

A few jurisdictions still host very primitive websites, offering little more than a list of offices at town hall. If yours is among them, it may be hard to determine where your problem fits in. In this case, do not hesitate to email or call whatever office seems to handle matters in the same ballpark. For example, it would be logical to pose your question about hazardous waste disposal to the environmental commission if there is no more appropriate link.

Tips and Techniques

Where do you start if your town has no online presence at all? You should be able to find basic local government materials at the nearest public library. But it is also a good idea to check the website of your county, which may provide links to sources of information about the municipalities within its borders.

Unfortunately, even the most comprehensive and business-friendly government website is not a one-stop shop for all the information you are likely to need to solve a problem. Here are six major shortcomings of these sites:

1. They are focused on what and how, not why. In other words, the website of your state's public health agency will list current and pending regulations, and describe how you can participate in the rule-making process. But it would be very unusual to find explanations either for the rules or for any of the agency's procedures.
2. In most cases, they are not oriented to any particular industry or occupation. This means you may sift through mountains of information that is generally applicable to small businesses without finding anything specifically relevant to you.
3. Even if specific questions are invited, it may take considerable time to get answers. Moreover, many officials will not be completely frank in writing (for fear that their words could become part of a legal proceeding or otherwise used against them).
4. The sites are not always up to date, especially with pending legislation or regulatory action. In particular, the names and titles of agency personnel may not be current.
5. Like the vast majority of other government documents, official websites rarely acknowledge mistakes.
6. They are written in government-speak. There is no reason why you can't master this wordy, ponderous language—in fact, one good reason to peruse these websites is to get accustomed to the jargon. But you can waste time scratching your head over a directive like this: "Pursuant to State Law XQ746912:403, this jurisdiction has specified a processing period during which duly authorized persons may request documents or other materials including but not limited to those immediately available to applicants or credentialed representatives at this or other sites." In English, this means: Expect to be asked for more paperwork.

Tips and Techniques

If something you learn about government flies in the face of your everyday experience, the problem may come down to a single word. More precisely, there may be a critical term that means one thing to those on the inside, and another to everyone else.

For example, some San Diego property owners were nonplussed by their city's official report that every pothole was "addressed" within 72 hours of being reported. Most waited much longer for repairs to get started—even scheduled.

It turned out that at city hall, "addressed" referred to a database designation, not a real-world fix. The word "repaired," too, had an idiosyncratic definition. According to one report: "The Street Division calculates its response time based on a number of factors that don't end up reflecting the common interpretation of the word 'repaired.' In some cases, the division considers a pothole to be repaired even though no work has been completed on the site. . . . The result is a performance measure that misleads residents and their City Council representatives."[2]

Lesson learned: Government-speak can endow the simplest words with incomprehensible meanings. If you are trying to figure out why something doesn't make sense, start by getting a clear definition of the terminology.

After doing as much as you can on official government sites, you can turn to these alternative online resources:

Media Archives

In today's wired world, many businesspeople don't make the time to read a daily newspaper, or believe they can get the same information elsewhere. Sometimes, they can. But skilled journalists add value—context, background, and fact-checking. Thoughtful editorials challenge conventional assumptions, helping readers develop well-informed points of view.

Whether or not you choose to be a regular reader, do not overlook the informational riches contained in newspaper (or magazine) archives. Although every media website is unique, it rarely takes more than a few keystrokes to access all recent reportage and commentary on any major topic. Some publications provide only abstracts (brief summaries) of stories more than a few weeks old, requiring payment to retrieve the full text. But that small fee may save you many hours of independent searching.

Tips and Techniques

Among the many online experiments now common in journalism is EveryBlock, a free compilation of hyper-local news and civic information. On a neighborhood-by-neighborhood level, it synthesizes media reportage, government proceedings, blogs, and other data. Even if this material is not exactly what you need, it can give you an overview of current issues and help you refine your own search. (Currently, EveryBlock is available only in major cities.)

Increasingly, radio and television stations also offer online archives. In broadcast media, these resources are commonly termed "on demand". A small local station may not routinely post this material, but often will provide it in some written form on request.

What about blogs? It's fine to peruse their archives too, but keep in mind that there is no editorial filter. Blogs can run the gamut from rigorous journalism to personal vendettas. Many are blatantly partisan; some habitually disguise political attacks as hard data. Before making a judgment about an unfamiliar blog, take a close look at the nature and tone of the posts. It can also be helpful to check the quality of other blogs linked to the one you are searching.

Reports and Publications Issued By Academic Institutions, Government Agencies, and Public Interest Organizations

A vast array of world-class scholarly investigations and analyses, once available only within the academic community, are now published online. They can originate with public and private universities, government research agencies, or public interest nonprofits. Some have a small cost, but many are free.

However, before using this material, you must try to make sure that the research was conducted or the analysis vetted by reputable groups. Remember that on the web, anyone can pose as an "expert." Here are a few indicators of quality:

- *A domain extension appropriate to the source.* Check for .edu (an academic institution), .gov (a public agency), or .org (a registered nonprofit). Of course, you cannot assume that a publication is flawless just because it has one of these imprimaturs; but at least you know that someone stands behind its basic veracity.
- *The author's credentials.* Even if a report is issued by a respected institution, its writer may simply be musing on issues beyond his expertise. Alternatively, he may be known for an unconventional perspective that you do not share. Review his biography and note his other works.
- *Links, footnotes, and other documentation.* What kinds of sites or other publications does this author refer to? Are they current? Reputable? Real? One-sided? If there are links, do they work? If there are footnotes, are they clear?

Political Literature

By its very nature, political literature (or broadcast material, like campaign commercials) is biased. Its assertions and denials can be over the top. But candidates craft this material to showcase what they see as their strongest positions. You should know if their beliefs align with yours.

You Tube and political blogs notwithstanding, political literature can be hard to find on the web after the election. If it is not available on the website of the candidate's political party, you will need to email either a party official or the candidate herself.

Now it's time to get out from behind your computer. Even the highest-quality cyber research can be vastly improved by a human touch. For example, you can:

Attend Public Meetings

Even streaming video cannot fully capture the tone and temperature of a meeting, or the personalities of participants. Especially if you plan to speak at a hearing at some future date, the best way to educate yourself about this type of forum is to attend one (or more.)

Talk to Knowledgeable People

Computers have not replaced human brains as repositories and processors of information. In many situations, the most important insights and advice are unpublished. They are, however, available for the asking from other businesspeople, government decision makers or bureaucrats who deal with matters related to yours. Check with your trade association, and put the word out on your professional and personal grapevines that you are seeking input. Don't hesitate to arrange fact-finding appointments at city hall.

Be Sensitive to Shifts in the Political and Economic Climate

A seemingly small change in the political landscape of your community or state can lead to seismic shifts in government. For example, if a governing body has a one-seat majority of Democrats, losing that single seat to a Republican will mean new priorities, appointments, and voting blocs. On the state level, the initiatives of a governor can be stymied by the opposition of just two or three leaders in the legislature.

Should the local economy turn sour, you are likely to find more sympathy for your business problems at the statehouse than when profits flowed like water. Conversely, an economic boom can stimulate public-private partnerships.

You cannot depend on news reports or disinterested analysis to alert you to political or economic climate change. Instead, you must pay attention to word of mouth; the behavior of community leaders; and tips or insights from your customers, vendors, and neighbors.

Go to the Library

At a minimum, almost all public libraries contain copies of municipal, county, and state "codes"—compilations of current laws and ordinances. More generally, an experienced librarian can be enormously valuable to a novice government researcher. She can steer you to emerging or little-known print and online resources; warn you about unreliable material; and help you wade through the dense terminology and complex indexing procedures common to the vast majority of official documents.

SECTION 2: HOW AND WHEN TO LOOK

Whatever the topic of your research, it should be guided by five principles:

Principle #1: Seek Clarity on the Parameters of Your Issue

Do not plunge blindly into the sea of government information until you know what you are diving for. In particular, you should know—or try to find out—who has authority in the matter that concerns you, and in what part of government.

Let's say your gift shop is cited by the municipal building department for violating a fire code regulation you never heard of. According to the letter, you must invest thousands of dollars to reconfigure the space. Angered, you rush to your computer determined to identify someone—anyone—with an email box at town hall. Without asking a single question about who is involved or why there is a problem, you pick the first name listed on the roster of the fire department, and shoot off a nasty note. Then you sit back, confident you will get an explanation for what you are sure is a mistake.

But you are already off track, for two reasons. First, in your town, enforcement of the fire code is under the jurisdiction of the building department. Most of the staff at the fire department are part-time, so it could take weeks until your email even gets forwarded to the right person. During that time, you could rack up additional penalties.

Second, in your state, the fire code itself is part of a set of uniform construction regulations stipulated by state law. Unbeknownst to you, the law was recently changed and your store is, in fact, in violation of the new standards. This means you need to lobby your state legislator to repeal or modify the law; perhaps he could advocate for a grandfather clause or a gradual phase-in of the changes. (Of course, you could still challenge the building inspector's report. But even if she made some technical error this time, it will not be long until she returns to check for the same violation.)

Here is another example. For years, you have sent your new employees to a computer education program at Big Town High School. Without warning, your latest group is turned away because they failed to bring proof of local residency. Outraged at this new requirement, you immediately call the president of the board of education, the mayor, and the governor to complain about pointless paperwork.

Although there is nothing wrong with making these calls, they are all misdirected. Big Town High School, like many others around the nation, receives funds from every level of government, but this particular program is an initiative of the county. To keep tuition low, the commissioners have decided to limit seats to county taxpayers—thus the reason for the new red tape. However, county officials will grant a waiver to employees of local businesses. You would have realized this if you'd read the notice of rejection more carefully before grabbing the phone.

Depending on your issue, it may not be easy to pinpoint the right people or level of government. But you can save a good deal of time by trying. Here are three suggestions:

1. If there is money involved, track where it goes. To whom are you expected to remit a payment? For what purpose? In the fire code scenario, your first clue might have been a statement that a fine has been incurred "pursuant to state law."
2. Think about who is affected by your issue. Although the computer education program is hosted by Big Town High School, it enrolls adults from all over Big County—and just from Big County. It is unlikely that such classes would be funded by the local board of education (which is focused on schoolchildren) or by the state (which only sponsors programs accessible to multiple counties).
3. Scrutinize the documentation. Sometimes the most obvious clues to where or with whom an issue originates are the ones you are least likely to notice: letterhead, titles, domain extensions, addresses, or stamps.

Principle #2: Clarify the Goal of Your Research

Depending on what you need to learn or how you intend to use the information you gather, here are three examples of different directions your research could take:

1. Are you primarily concerned with a process, or with a person?

Researching a process, like how to apply for a license or bid on a contract, is usually straightforward. If some aspect is not fully explained on the jurisdiction's website or if forms are not download-able, you can readily identify whom to call or where to go for more information. Do not hesitate to request an informational meeting with officials who administer the process; often they will share tips and insights that no one has thought to publish.

But researching a person is more complicated. On a state website, how much you can learn about a key decision maker will depend on what office he holds. For the most part, profiles of individuals in the executive branch (such as the governor, lieutenant governor, and audi-tor) and in the judicial branch (judges and other court officials) will be either bare-bones or hyperbolic. Typically, you will find next to noth-ing about lower-level officials (not even their names). However, if you are researching lawmakers, most state sites contain a treasure trove of insights. There will be biographies, committee assignments, and partisan leadership positions; most revealing, you will find each legislator's voting record, what bills he has sponsored and how many of his bills have become law. From this information, you can easily get a sense of his interests, priorities, and overall effectiveness in representing your interests. In addition, many state sites now live-stream and archive webcasts of legislative sessions, so you can watch him in action and judge for yourself how passionate and well informed he is about your issue.

Getting to know a county or municipal decision maker online is a bigger challenge. Again, you should start with the jurisdiction's website. But because few local sites make it easy to learn more than an official wishes to tell you, it will be necessary to do some digging. Although voting records will exist in some form, they may or may not be logically organized online. Importantly, you should also look for the minutes (or recordings) of public meetings to see what comments have been made about your issue. If this information is unavailable on the site, out of date, or not easily retrievable, a call to city hall should get you what you're missing.

Whether the person you are researching is a state or local official, you can fill in the blanks of their background by turning to media archives. A skilled journalist is able to capture a subject's temperament as well as her actions. Pay particular attention to direct quotes: what an official says, asks, criticizes, and defends in public is a window onto both her opinions and her personality. Additionally, if your subject is elected by the voters (not appointed by other officials), be sure to read accounts of her most recent campaign. Did she make promises related to your issue, or to business issues in general? Was she endorsed by business groups? If her campaign literature is accessible, it can be enlightening to read her own twist on your issue. Most elected officials (and certain appointed officials, depending on the state) are required to disclose lists of their political donors and expenditures; check with the board of elections to learn how to access this data. Some jurisdictions also require disclosure of personal financial records.

2. Are you seeking background data to incorporate into a document or public comment?

Perhaps you are preparing testimony for a public hearing, or writing a letter to the editor of a local newspaper. Instead of describing only your own problem, you will make a bigger impact by citing statistics or the experiences of other businesspeople.

In this situation, you should search for reports and publications issued on your topic by academic institutions, government agencies, or public interest organizations. Let's say you want to address economic opportunities in Maryland: Johns Hopkins University's Institute for Policy Studies publishes papers on many aspects of the regional economy. Do you hope to make a case for business development in Arizona? A good place to start would be the Arizona Workforce Informer, a website produced by the state's Department of Commerce Research Administration.

Tips and Techniques

Do not be afraid to rely on the research of a public interest organization just because you don't share the group's political leanings or general ideology. For example, the Institute for Justice describes itself as "a libertarian public interest law firm." Whether or not libertarianism is to your liking, the group issues well-documented reports on subjects like eminent domain and occupational regulation.

---

3. Do you want to know the reason why a law was passed, or a regulation enacted?

You will not find this kind of information on a government website. Turn to media archives, political or government watchdog blogs, or the campaign literature of the officials who supported or opposed the law/regulation.

Of course, the best way to understand someone's thinking is to ask him. If you can identify the key sponsor of the law or supporter of the regulation, you should not hesitate to call his office, or approach him at a meeting. He may be unwilling to speak frankly about his position—but that reaction, in itself, would be revealing.

Principle #3: At Least at the Start of Your Research, Be Open-Minded

It's natural to have at least a few preconceptions, but you should not let them get ahead of you. For instance, if you know someone who had a bad experience when seeking a building permit, it's a mistake to assume you will, too. Research the application procedures and evaluate your chances objectively; better yet, get advice from the building department. Do not waste time looking for ways to beat the system when you don't even understand how it works.

Principle #4: Don't Give Up

Too many businesspeople are easily intimidated by public officials. When asking questions or looking for data, they allow themselves to be distracted, blown off, or simply ignored. Do not let this happen to you. Remember, as a taxpayer, you are the ultimate employer of everyone on the government payroll. From the loftiest to the lowliest, their work product belongs to you. It never helps to be nasty; if a staffer tells you that it will take a lot of time to fulfill your request, you will not get anything faster by yelling at her. But you shouldn't apologize for asking, or hesitate to follow up. (If there is a legitimate reason to withhold information, it must be explained to you.)

Principle #5: Timing Matters

Doing your research at the right time can be as important as doing it the right way. As a general rule, you should avoid much data-gathering just before or just after an election. Unless the outcome is certain—and it almost never is—a lot of basic information, like who is in charge of what, will be subject to change with a new administration. (This holds true on every level of government, from Washington to the tiniest town.)

Certain kinds of information must be current when you use them. For example, as part of your testimony against a new labor regulation, it would make sense to cite unemployment statistics. But you will look foolish if the numbers are months old. So you should collect such data as late as possible in the research process, and assure officials that you took pains to bring them the most up-to-date information.

Tips and Techniques

If your topic is time-sensitive and you are using an unfamiliar website, be cautious about how (or whether) the information is dated. Some sites regularly change the date at the bottom of their home page, but this does not mean that all the data is current. Cached pages, in particular, can be tricky; try checking references or footnotes to get some sense of when the material was actually written.

On the other hand, there could be times when you need to rush your research. Perhaps a key resource person is leaving his job, or a department is being cut. More often, it will be because you need to meet a deadline. In the administrative rule-making process, for instance, the most compelling plea may be ignored just because it was submitted after the public comment period ended.

SECTION 3. GETTING SPECIFIC

On your computer or elsewhere in your office, there is undoubtedly a compilation of key information about your business. It might explain, for example, how to contact your attorney and accountant, where to order supplies, and who to call if the copy machine breaks down.

Basic information about state and local government should be just as handy. If you collect it when you don't have a serious problem, you won't need to scramble—and potentially make mistakes—when you do. Moreover, this information can make your business life easier in ways you never imagined.

Here are the specific facts and resources you should always have at your fingertips:

1. The structure of your county and municipal governments.

State governments look, and operate, pretty much alike. But as you learned in Chapter Three, counties and municipalities can be very different. Knowing the structural characteristics of your hometown government is not just of academic interest. It will tell you where the power lies, and who is most likely to be responsive to a particular type of business or issue.

Which of the major governance systems—mayor-council, council-manager, or commission—is used by your city or town? Is your mayor weak or strong? If you have a strong mayor in a mayor-council government, she calls the shots and should be at the top of your list of town hall contacts. But a weak mayor in a mayor-council system is only as effective as the council allows her to be. Here you would need to know the names of the councilpersons. It is important to find out if a particular council member represents your neighborhood, because that person would be most concerned about your business. (If the council-persons are elected at-large, this means that all of them represent the entire community. But it is still worth asking if they champion different issues or specialize in different kinds of problems.)

In a commission system, there will be a clear delineation of responsibilities. For example, if people were parking illegally in your lot, you would call the commissioner who heads the police department. But if you want to construct more parking spaces, you need to know who is in charge of the building department. Many counties also use a commission system, though there are regional variations.

Dealing with a council-manager government can be tricky. You should definitely learn how to contact the manager, as he is the chief administrator and has the most wide-ranging power to get things done. However, he is not directly accountable to voters and may not go out of his way to be helpful to individual businesses. That doesn't mean you should not reach out to him if you have a problem; in fact, it would be a big mistake not to try. But, to cover all your bases, you should be prepared to communicate simultaneously with each member of the council.

You should also be aware of the partisan makeup of the government. Whether or not you are involved with local politics, it can't help to be ignorant of which party is in power and what ideology is ascendant in your state, county, and town.

Finally, remember to check on nitty-gritty details: locations, hours, and parking facilities at different government offices. You might also need to know where and when there is access to notaries public or translators.

2. What troubleshooting and/or educational resources are available.

State and local governments have not stopped imposing regulations and red tape on small businesses, but an increasing number have acknowledged that it is in everyone's interest to smooth the compliance process. A decade ago, you would have been on your own in deciphering forms and wading through paperwork. Today there are small business ombudsmen and service centers in communities of every size, staffed by trained counselors whose sole responsibility is to help ordinary people hack through the jungle of government. Some are online; others maintain a physical presence.

At the state level, look for a Small Business Development Center, sponsored by the U.S. Small Business Administration as a clearinghouse of information and a central site for education and advice about federal, state, and local government. The SBA also offers the Business Gateway Program (accessed through the website Business.gov), an online small business community combining articles, blogs, and discussion threads.

Some states also run their own programs. For example, Rhode Island's Every Company Counts offers free one-on-one consultations with business experts. South Carolina's Business One Stop is a web portal providing custom online tutorials. The Massachusetts Business Resource Team matches companies' needs to state programs. Virginia's Electronic Commerce Assistance helps get small and medium-size firms ready to do business online.

A wide and creative array of business assistance services have begun to crop up in cities and towns. Corridors of Opportunity in Louisville, Kentucky helps retailers to find sites, and developers to find tenants. The Economic Gardening Program in Littleton, Colorado, aids entrepreneurs with free direct marketing lists, maps of potential markets, and model business plans. In Memphis, Tennessee, the Fast Track Program expedites review of building plans, while in Manchester, Connecticut, Small Business Nights offer evening consultations with building officials about code, engineering, zoning, and other regulations.

It will not be hard to learn what your community offers. Whether or not you need these resources right away, just knowing they exist can spare you anxiety in the future.

Tips and Techniques

It is possible that your search for business assistance services will find nothing convenient to your area or relevant to your needs. Don't give up. Discuss this deficiency with your trade association or other local businesspeople; together, you could ask community officials to consider starting a program modeled on others you have researched.

---

3. What free or low-cost products are sold or given away.

Are you planning to landscape your property? Don't buy mulch or wood chips before asking if your town offers them for free. To save on their own disposal costs, many municipal public works facilities are glad to give away this detritus of their spring cleaning or snow removal operations. Find out when your local public library gives away boxes of old books to clear the shelves for bestsellers: It's the perfect opportunity to fill your office bookcase.

While researching local government giveaways, be sure to collect information about auctions of surplus public property. You can bid on millions of dollars worth of used, seized, and unclaimed furniture, equipment, vehicles, artwork, and many other items. Because the government does not try to make money on these sales, you can typically get rock-bottom prices.

Also, don't overlook all the free advice available from government experts, not just about running a business but on other cost-saving topics like cutting energy consumption.

4. What e-forms and e-processes are available.

The federal government has pioneered several e-initiatives to help small businesses understand and connect with its departments and agencies. For example, Regulations.gov is an online portal where you can find, read, and comment on rules proposed by federal agencies and departments. Business.gov offers a wide variety of resources and links, ranging from help with filing a regulatory complaint to primers on business law.

Although e-connections are also multiplying rapidly at other levels of government, there is still enormous variation around the country. You must research what is available from your town, county, and state—including any special software or tutorials needed to access a particular filing or application system.

5. What e-alerts you can receive.

It isn't necessary to reinvent the wheel every time you need certain types of information. For example, if you hope to become a government vendor, you could spend time every week combing through published bid lists, but many purchasing departments will place you on an e-notification list which will alert you to relevant opportunities. Do you need to stay on top of the status of a proposed regulation? Ask the relevant agency to send you their e-newsletter or put you on other automatic update lists.

6. How to report crime or public corruption.

If you have witnessed what you believe to be a crime, you should contact the office of the top law enforcement official in the appropriate jurisdiction; usually, this will be a district attorney, county prosecutor, or state attorney general.

To report government waste, fraud, misconduct, mismanagement, or potential corruption, use the whistleblower mechanism offered in your community. For problems involving a federal employee or program, the U.S. SBA provides an online complaint submission form. On a local level, you will often find an anonymous telephone hotline. One example: The Network in Tulsa, Oklahoma, receives calls around the clock and guides callers through the reporting process.

A final note: When starting your research, don't be tempted to waste money on commercial publications that are nothing but print-outs of public information easily accessible for free. Also, be wary of "consultants" who offer to expedite basic government processes. It might be cost-effective to hire a compliance expert or a regulatory facilitator in some industries, such as those with unusually complex environmental impacts or licensing requirements. But in the vast majority of cases, anyone who is smart enough to run a small business is perfectly capable of navigating government.

KEY POINTS TO REMEMBER

- Because there is no one-stop shop for all the information you are likely to need, it is important to be aware of and open to the full array of resources—both online and offline.
- Do not expect any source of information to be flawless, or equally appropriate to every situation.
- Efficient research requires a specific goal, clear parameters, and appropriate timing.
- It is well worth the time to compile basic information about state and local government when you don't have a problem—so you won't need to scramble when you do.

NOTES

1. H. Boyd, R. Westfall, and S. Stasch, *Marketing Research: Text and Cases*, 6th ed. (R. Irwin: Homewood, IL, 1985), p. 5.

2. K. Kyle, "The City's False Pothole Pledge," December 14, 2009, voiceofsandiego.org.

6

Get Smart II: Advanced Research

OVERVIEW

Basic research is like the foundation of a building: Once completed, it can support many different architectural elements. Similarly, now that you have a solid base—or know how to create one—you are ready to take advantage of other techniques.

Of course, it is not always necessary to go beyond the basics. To answer routine questions, you may already have amassed enough information. But it can take a lot of digging to get to the bottom of a regulatory or red tape problem. Dealing with public corruption can involve much more than filing a complaint.

That's why you should be familiar with additional research options. In general, these will cost more, both in time and in money, than basic information-gathering methods. But as with any other business skill, the more research you do, the more efficiently you will do it. Also, in the course of applying these techniques, you may meet new people, open new doors, and identify new directions for your advocacy— and for your business.

Section 1: Freedom of Information Requests

Although government disseminates a great deal of information as a matter of course, you may need data that is collected but unpublished. Here is how to go about getting it.

Section 2: Doing a Survey

Sometimes the information you need simply does not exist. If it is vital to making your case, you should consider using a survey to collect it.

Section 3: Getting Help

Depending on what you are researching, it may be possible to attract a collaborator. This section discusses the types of issues most likely to appeal to journalists, public interest organizations, government officials, and political candidates.

Section 4: Getting Started

Constructing a simple list at the start of your project can help you sort out and select various research techniques.

* * *

SECTION 1: FREEDOM OF INFORMATION REQUESTS

Let's say you had a run-in with the health department inspector newly assigned to your restaurant. He got angry when you challenged his observations, cutting you off when you tried to respond and even accusing you of falsifying records. So it came as no surprise when his report was extremely unfavorable. Unless you contest the findings, you will face thousands of dollars in fines.

But before you put up a fight, you want to show that this inspector has a history of bad behavior. In fact, you've heard on the grapevine that he is known for persecuting restaurateurs he doesn't like, slamming them, on average, with twice as many violations as any other sanitarian. You are confident that this discrepancy can be documented by simply comparing a year's worth of his reports to those of other inspectors.

Then you learn that your town does not publish individual restaurant inspection reports, either by inspector or by establishment. The only information on the health department's website is a composite set of statistics. Have you reached a dead end?

You are not at an end, but at a beginning. It is time to learn how to exercise one of your lesser known but critical rights as a citizen. Whether or not information is published by federal, state, or local government—if it pertains to public business, you are entitled to it.

From the earliest days of the Republic, American leaders have recognized that freedom of information is central to democracy. Throughout our history, officials in every city and state have reaffirmed the right of citizens to know where their money is spent, what decisions are made on their behalf, and how their government operates.

During a debate on the floor of the U.S. Senate in 1792, Elbridge Gerry of Massachusetts warned his colleagues that transparency is fundamental to democracy: "However firmly liberty may be established in any country, it cannot long subsist if the channels of information be stopped." At least one other senator needed no convincing. Added James Madison: "In such [a government] as ours, where members are so far removed from the eye of their constituents, an easy and prompt circulation of public proceedings is peculiarly essential."

But it is one thing to proclaim a principle, and another to put it into practice. Information disclosure was spotty until 1966, when the Freedom of Information (FOI) law standardized the responsibilities and procedures of every federal agency. FOI specified exactly what types of records must be made available as a matter of routine, either in print or (thanks to a 1996 amendment) online. The law also guaranteed every citizen's right to request copies of information not normally disseminated to the public. Although FOI allowed agencies to withhold certain material from disclosure, such as medical records or military secrets, it provided a mechanism to appeal any denial.

Today, if you are seeking public records from Washington, the website of the U.S. Department of Justice is an excellent, citizen-friendly place to start. It offers not only a wide-ranging collection of FOI guidelines and recommendations, but referrals to a myriad of FOI resources elsewhere. Other federal agencies also maintain their own FOI websites, with agency-specific information. For example, the Securities and Exchange Commission explains that an FOI request is required to obtain the record of an investigation, but not to read the decision resulting from that investigation. If you are denied information for what you believe is an inappropriate reason, you may ask for your case to be reviewed by the FOI ombudsman, housed in the National Archives and Records Administration.

Tips and Techniques

To get a feel for the range of data sets generated by the federal
government, visit Data.gov, an easy-to-use introduction to this
vast array of public information. The customized search engine,
Search.USA.gov, can help you home in on your topic.

However, FOI does not apply to state and local governments—
precisely where small businesses are most likely to need help. The good
news is that all 50 states, and many counties and municipalities, have
their own laws guaranteeing access to public documents and meetings.
The bad news: these laws are not uniformly effective. Procedures are
sometimes cumbersome or unclear. Compliance may be grudging: a
2008 audit by the Florida Society of Newspaper Editors, for instance,
found a 43 percent non-compliance rate among local officials in 56
counties.[1] Worse, many businesspeople don't know the laws exist;
when seeking information about government, they take "no" for an
answer when they have every right to a "yes."

This section began by describing a situation where unpublished
government information could be crucial to a small (or any size) business. The number of these situations is almost limitless. To give you a
sense of their diversity, here are other examples:

- You are evaluating a former industrial building for sale by a public
  agency. The agency claims it has completed all required environmental cleanups. However, you want to compare the contaminants
  found on this property to those found elsewhere in the city. To do
  this, you need environmental records from nearby sites.
- Your customers often park in metered spaces on Main Street. But
  many complain that they are ticketed before their meters run out.
  You believe that police are deliberately discouraging on-street parking to steer more cars into your competitors' lots. To bolster your
  complaint, you want to review records of how many parking tickets
  are routinely issued elsewhere in the city.
- The county's road reconstruction project is blocking the front of your
  office. It is way behind schedule and far more disruptive to local traffic than officials had estimated. When you complain, you are told to
  be patient—or erect a temporary entrance. But if county engineers

made mistakes, you should not have to pay for them. To document those errors, you need to read internal projections and analyses.

- You bid on a municipal consulting contract several times, only to be told that other vendors were better qualified. You suspect that your competitors offered not superior credentials, but outsize political donations. If this is true, it may constitute a crime. You can look for evidence by reviewing their contracts together with campaign disclosures.

If you have a need for hard-to-access government information, here are the steps to take—and the tripwires to prepare for.

Step 1

Learn your rights and responsibilities under the freedom of information laws in your state or local government. Start by checking online resources; if there is no category called "freedom of information," search for terms like *open government* or *sunshine laws*. Look for at least these four guidelines: who is entitled to what information, how requests should be made, how much time is allowed for a response to your request, and how to appeal if your request is denied. Download any sample text or formats (even if you don't use them, these materials will help you understand what officials want). Keep in mind that different levels of government may have different forms, fees, and transmittal instructions. For instance, your town may accept information requests by phone, while the county insists on written formats.

Some websites are highly interactive and easy to use. For example, New Jersey allows the public to submit FOI requests to different state agencies from a central portal. Some cities, like Seattle, also offer on-line public disclosure request forms. Web-based educational resources can be extensive: Oregon provides an especially comprehensive, downloadable "Citizens Guide to Public Records and Meetings."

But some local governments can make the process of requesting information more complicated than the information itself. The website may post little more than a cursory reference to the law, or nothing. Where instructions exist, they can be confusing. It may be hard to identify who, if anyone, is responsible for compliance within a particular agency or department. Officials may subtly communicate that they want you—and your request—to go away.

Don't get discouraged. Remember, just as businesses must comply with regulations whether they like them or not, so must the government. If you cannot find what you need on a state website, call the office of the governor or the attorney general. Although the implementation of FOI may fall under the auspices of another official—in Ohio, for instance, it is the auditor of state—ultimate responsibility for enforcing these laws rests with the top executives.

If you are stymied by a county or municipality, contact the chief administrator or clerk. Alternatively, you could reach out to the mayor or any other elected official. Don't worry that such a call would be rebuffed. Mayor Jones will recognize you're doing her a favor by alerting her to her constituents' need for easier disclosure!

Step 2

Determine what to ask for. This is trickier than it sounds. As a general rule, although officials must provide information, they are not required to sort, compile, summarize, or analyze it. This means that you may need to request material in a form less convenient or comprehensive than you might have liked.

Let's say you hope to determine how many city contracts a certain political donor received after the last three elections. But the city organizes its contract award records by year instead of by name. Because officials are not obligated to extract data relating to an individual vendor, you would have to ask for the last three years' worth of contract records and comb through them yourself.

In another example, you want a record of all the building permits issued in a redevelopment district. However, many permits go to developers' post office boxes, so they cannot be linked to a street. To achieve your goal, you would need to obtain the address of every new building in the district, determine the name of each developer, and then get the list of every permit issued to that name.

This illustrates another point: an FOI request can take much more of your time than you expect. So before going this route, make sure you have exhausted all other options. Did you try available search engines? Have you asked your trade association? Did you check a wide array of newspaper archives? In many cases, even if something is not posted on an official website, a polite phone call to the right person will get results (return to the previous chapter to learn how to identify that person).

> **Tips and Techniques**
>
> Here is another way to minimize time and aggravation spent on unnecessary FOI requests: Ask yourself whether the information, when or if you get it, will really change anything. Take the example at the beginning of this section. If you intend to challenge the inspector's report—and demand a new inspection—regardless of what the research turns up, why do it?

Step 3

Determine how to ask. This is another often-unforeseen FOI challenge. That's because of the language gap: You are likely to state the information you want in simple, colloquial terms that don't match how a government office describes or stores it. A request that seems straightforward to you can end up being ambiguous or vague to the person who, with the best of intentions, tries to fulfill it.

Here is what can happen. You want to review the prices paid by your town for computer monitors over the last five years. So in the "record description" space on the FOI form, you write "town computer bills—five years." After weeks of delay, you get hundreds of pages of invoices for hardware, software, supplies, service, and other expenditures related to computers but of no interest to you. Depending on how the FOI official interprets your request, you might get only those bills attached to five-year contracts—or even a huge pile of all the town's computer-generated bills.

This would be bad enough if the only result was wasted paper. But a poorly crafted FOI request can mean big, unanticipated copying costs—not to mention exasperation on both sides. In some states, the law also allows local jurisdictions to charge you for the labor involved in reproducing the material (and as a taxpayer you pay for it a second time, indirectly.)

How can you know the best way to phrase your request? In most cases, you can't. Instead of guessing, call the appropriate agency and explain the goal of your research. Although not all FOI administrators are equally responsive, most realize that they help themselves by helping you. Government does not make money on this service: It is in everyone's interest to make the process as smooth as possible. In fact, there are many proactive officials who will take the initiative to reach out to you if they suspect your request needs clarification. Never be defensive—be grateful.

Step 4

Follow up. Most FOI laws stipulate a maximum response time, so the process cannot drag on forever. But it can be significantly delayed by a time-intensive request, a backlog in the office, a copier breakdown, or for a myriad of other legitimate reasons.

In any case, it never hurts to be persistent—and it can help if your follow-up query alerts you to a problem like ambiguity or potentially exorbitant copying costs. If you suspect that someone mishandled or forgot your request, ask—politely—to talk with their supervisor. As with all other interactions with government, you will get further with courtesy than curtness.

Tips and Techniques

In case you're wondering if FOI laws are taken seriously, be assured that they are vigorously enforced in the vast majority of state and local jurisdictions. While it is uncommon for disclosure disputes to go to court, this is a viable option—though obviously a last resort. Under normal circumstances, you don't need an attorney to file an information request.

SECTION 2: DOING A SURVEY

Occasionally a research effort can be diligent but fruitless. What if you know precisely what information you need—but you have learned that it doesn't exist?

Sometimes you can gather the information yourself. This is called *primary research*. Its methods vary enormously in complexity and cost, but even a beginner can design and field the most basic primary research tool: a survey.

Let's say you are pushing to change a severely restrictive downtown parking regulation just imposed by Mayor Smith. Based on what you have learned about him, you believe Smith would repeal the new law if you could show him evidence that it is hurting most local stores.

Specifically, you need to document a decline in the number of their customers since the regulation went into effect. How could you get this information?

One way is to hire a local polling firm or online consultant. If you are extremely pressed for time (or could persuade other businesses to share the cost) this might be a good investment. But if you are able to make the effort, you can produce some reasonable data yourself. Here are the five steps to follow:

1. Decide exactly what you need to know.

The key to minimizing your time and any costs of the survey is to focus tightly on what is essential to make your case. For example, it might be interesting to ask business owners their overall opinion of Mayor Smith, but this information would be irrelevant to the regulatory issue.

Also, do not try to use the survey as a sales tool. Potential customers might appreciate your efforts to ease downtown parking, but this is not the appropriate venue to seek feedback about your brand.

2. Develop questions.

As a rule, the shorter the better. Use simple, everyday words—if you must include government jargon or acronyms, explain what they mean. Avoid ambiguity: If you ask about "frequent" downtown shoppers, for instance, define "frequent" in objective terms like "Makes purchases at least twice a week."

More generally, beware of these common pitfalls:

- Too many questions. Again, focus is critical. People get bored with a long list of survey questions, and will respond more thoughtfully if you don't impose on their time.
- Unproductive questions. Whatever the answers, certain questions won't be useful. If your goal is to change a parking regulation, there is no reason to ask "Do you feel there is too much competition downtown?" Unless you plan to run against Mayor Smith, what is the purpose of asking "Do you believe our mayor is incompetent?"
- Leading questions. You should give respondents an opportunity to express their opinions, not lead them to a predetermined conclusion. Consider: "Do you believe free downtown parking would give a big boost to your bottom line?" This question cannot be answered clearly by anyone who a) thinks free parking might help, but only slightly, or b) is not sure.

- Double-barreled questions. These lump two different issues together. For example: "Do you agree that changing this regulation and other city codes would help your business?" What if respondents want to change the parking code but are satisfied with the others?

If possible, try to use closed-ended (multiple choice) instead of open-ended response options. This will make it much easier to compare and analyze the total pool of responses. For example, if you ask "How many product lines does your store sell?" and provide a line to write in any answer, people might reasonably respond "Lots of different brands" or "More than any of my competitors." You will get cleaner data by asking them to check a category like "More than a dozen" or "Fewer than 5."

3. Choose respondents and a method of reaching them.

The gold standard in survey research is a randomized sample, selected from the target population in such a way as to ensure statistically accurate representation of the group as a whole. Getting a truly random sample is difficult and costly.

Fortunately, it is unnecessary for your purposes. You simply need to be clear about whose opinions you need and how you can easily reach them. To do the parking regulation survey, your target group would include all downtown businesses affected by the regulation; you would exclude residences or firms with private parking lots.

Now let's assume you have access to both email and postal mail addresses for every target business. Which should you use? Emailing a questionnaire is easy, fast, and essentially cost-free. But many people hate unsolicited email. They are likely to delete your survey without even glancing at it. To improve response rates, it would be important to choose an attention-getting subject line and include a clear explanation of how this survey could help their business.

Although postal mail may be perceived as less intrusive than email, it is easily discarded or ignored. Again, a compelling introduction would help; so would a postage-paid envelope. Overall, this is the more expensive approach, but sometimes it is more effective than email in breaking through the clutter. (To help choose which is best for your particular target, you might ask the advice of a chamber of commerce or trade group.)

If you can't get a complete list of addresses, you could do the survey over the phone. But this is extremely time-consuming. Also, many people have been soured by telemarketers posing as pollsters, and will refuse to participate.

Another option is to personally deliver your questionnaire to each respondent. Of course, this is practical only if their number is manageable. But if it is, the human touch is likely to get you the best participation of all.

4. Analyze your results.

Survey data can be entered into an Excel sheet or analyzed by any type of statistical software. Most of these programs will perform standard manipulations like frequencies and cross tabulations.

You could also weigh the costs and benefits of using a web survey site. These offer highly sophisticated analyses and display devices.

Tips and Techniques

Although online survey firms charge for many services, the major sites also provide free, high-quality educational materials and questionnaire-building tools. Five examples: SurveyMonkey, Poll-Cat, QuestionPro, Zoomerang, and The Survey System.

SECTION 3: GETTING HELP

Sometimes you can convince a journalist, public interest organization, government official, or political candidate to help with your research—even to do it themselves. The key is to understand your potential partner's perspective and self-interest.

Journalists are valuable allies, because they are specially trained to dig beneath the surface of government for information not normally released to the public. But to get their attention, there must be a potential story: In other words, the project must break new ground or promise a fresh angle on a significant issue. Corruption is a particularly enticing topic for an investigative reporter, assuming you can bring her well-grounded suspicions or preliminary evidence.

Public interest groups don't necessarily care if information is newsworthy as long as it advances their cause. A local environmental organization might jump at the chance to follow up on your concerns about contamination at downtown building sites. Even a national group could take an interest in your case; for example, the Institute for Justice pursues problems with occupational licensing and other regulations in many different municipalities and states.

A government official could pick up on your research if he is developing related legislation or policy ideas. How can you find a good prospect? Go back to your basic research: This is the kind of lead to look for as you are reading media archives, attending public meetings, or talking to people who are familiar with an official's priorities.

A political candidate could be eager to pursue your issue if it puts her opponent in a bad light. However, you must be cautious: Before trying this approach, use the suggestions in Chapter Three to become familiar with the political landscape. In particular, you need to steer clear of any candidate whose methods or goals might be dubious. And keep in mind that if your issue takes on a partisan slant, you may alienate other potential allies.

Tips and Techniques

If you decide to approach a political candidate, decide whether you are comfortable having your name publicly associated with the campaign. Whether or not you give permission, the connection is likely to leak out.

SECTION 4: GETTING STARTED

Depending on your problem, you can experiment with any number of basic or advanced research techniques, alone or in combination. But to avoid wasting time (and, potentially, money) you need a research plan. Begin by writing down the goals of your research. List each type of information you need, and then match it with the various research methods that could help unearth that information. Make choices based on how much time you have, how much money you can spend, and whether you have research partners. Here are examples:

Problem: Red Tape

Research Goal: To identify who or what caused the bottleneck; reasonable administrative alternatives; and who has authority to make modifications or exemptions.

First type of information needed: Names and procedures (Who are the administrative decision makers? Which elected officials have jurisdiction? What are the formal appeal procedures?)

Techniques: Website search, phone calls.

Second type of information needed: What is the informal advice of administrative officials?

Technique: Informational meetings.

Third type of information needed: What is the advice of other businesspeople?

Techniques: Solicit input from your personal network; talk to knowledgeable people.

Fourth type of information needed: What is the actual (documented) experience of other businesspeople?

Techniques: FOI request; reports issued by institutions or organizations; survey.

Fifth type of information needed: Might an elected official take up your cause?

Techniques: Media archives; public meetings (attend and/or review minutes); talk to knowledgeable people; read campaign literature.

Problem: Regulation

Research Goal: To understand the status of the regulation; its legislative history; its impact on other businesses; and who calls the shots at the regulatory agency.

First type of information needed: Names and procedures (Who are the agency decision makers? What stage of the rule-making process has been reached? What avenues for comment are or will become available to you?)

Techniques: Website search, phone calls.

Second type of information needed: What is the informal advice of regulatory officials?

Technique: Informational meetings.

Third type of information needed: Which legislators have been champions (or opponents) of this regulation?

Techniques: Media archives; talk to knowledgeable people.

Fourth type of information needed: Are there legislative remedies?

Techniques: Informational meetings (with one or more of the legislators who have a history with this regulatory issue).

Fifth type of information needed: What is the experience and advice of other businesspeople?

Techniques: Media archives; reports issued by organizations or institutions; solicit information from your personal network; talk to knowledgeable people; survey.

Problem: Corruption

Research Goal: To protect yourself and potentially expose wrongdoing.

First type of information needed: Names and procedures (Who are the law enforcement authorities in the jurisdiction? What type of whistleblower mechanism or ethics hotline is available?)

Technique: Website search, phone calls.

Second type of information needed: Background information about the suspected lawbreaker.

Techniques: Media archives; campaign finance disclosures; personal disclosures; talk to knowledgeable people; FOI request.

Third type of information needed: Have other citizens observed the suspicious behavior?

Techniques: Solicit input from your personal network; talk to knowledgeable people.

KEY POINTS TO REMEMBER

- Before getting started, develop a research plan.
- If the information you need is not readily available—for any reason—don't give up. Think about creative ways to find or generate it.
- Before plunging into a challenging research project on your own, consider approaching potential partners.
- Remember: You have a right to access (almost) any government records.

NOTE

1. A. Palm, "Want Public Records in Florida? Get Ready for a Hassle," *Palm Beach Post*, March 15, 2010, www.palmbeachpost.com.

7

Speak Up I: Communication Tools

OVERVIEW

Too many small businesspeople, once burned by government, react by playing ostrich. They stick their heads in the sand, keep quiet, ignore public proceedings, and hope they will somehow drop off the radar screen.

They won't. Worse, by pretending to be ignorant about government, they will increase their chances of actually making a mistake. When the time comes to ask questions or seek help—as it inevitably will—they won't know how, where, or with whom to start.

Reticence is never the best strategy when dealing with government. Although speaking up does not ensure success, a lack of communication can guarantee failure. That's because the advocacy marketplace is extremely competitive: If you are absent from the marketplace of messages, someone else will take your place.

Moreover, if you make the effort to communicate, you will find that most public officials pay attention. When state legislators were asked in a survey about the origin of their policy ideas, the majority cited constituent input as extremely influential. One respondent commented: " 'The public underestimates what a difference one person can make in coming to their lawmaker with a problem. *A lot* of laws enacted begin with a constituent phone call or letter to a legislator. *A lot*.' "[1]

When your firm has a need for marketing communication, you don't just do whatever worked last time: You know that one tool, like an email, may be appropriate in one situation but less effective than a personal sales pitch or phone call in another. In the same way, different communication tools are available to help you interact with government. The better you understand the array of alternatives, the more likely you will select—and know how to use—precisely the right one.

Section 1: Written Tools

This section explains when and how to use email, postal mail, testimony, petitions, and blogs.

Section 2: Personal Contacts

Even if written materials are the backbone of your effort, there may still be an important role for one-on-one contact: phone calls or personal meetings.

Section 3: Communicating Through the Media

Print or broadcast media vehicles can amplify your voice to a level nearly impossible to achieve on your own. The catch: You cannot control how the media filters or interprets your message.

Section 4: Applications

Here you will find examples of how to combine different tools to deal with regulation, corruption, or red tape.

* * *

SECTION 1: WRITTEN TOOLS

"Put it in writing" is a common admonition in business, but it is even more critical when dealing with regulations, corruption, or red tape. Here are five reasons:

1. So many different people are likely to be involved.

   As described in Chapter One, the number of bureaucrats dealing with your issue at any given time will almost always be more than you expect. By documenting who is in the loop, you help to clarify the situation for everyone.

2. You may need to interact with overlapping jurisdictions.

   Again, bureaucratic complexity is a fact of government life. When there is a written record of who is responsible for what, there will be fewer people reinventing wheels or working at cross-purposes.

3. In government, nothing ever happens as fast as you hope.

A written record will quickly bring everyone up to speed when the time lapses—between conversations and other interactions—become significant.

4. There can be legal ramifications of who says what.

For the protection of everyone, it is always a good idea to have proof.

5. Certain processes require documentation.

For example, most FOI requests must be made in writing. To participate fully in administrative rule making, you will need to submit written comments in the form and time frame established by the agency. In some jurisdictions, a petition is not valid unless written in a required format and accompanied by a minimum number of signatures.

More generally, written words have staying power. They can be stored, shared, excerpted, reproduced, analyzed, and relied upon in ways that verbal communication cannot.

Let's say your state's environmental agency is about to set a new recycling rule, yet another costly headache for your company. During a meeting with a lawmaker, you explain your concerns and ask him to pass them along to the rule makers. The conversation may well be very useful; for instance, it may deter this official from supporting future disposal restrictions. But there is no guarantee that he will accurately convey your thoughts to the environmental officials. In fact, because he is busy and distracted by many other problems, he may not talk to them at all. By submitting written comments directly to the agency, you cannot be assured of derailing the new rule—but at least you will know your input was expressed correctly to the right people. Check the Appendix for models of regulatory comments.

Another reason to put your case in writing: It is easier for opponents to misrepresent or challenge a verbal exchange than a document. This is especially important in a dispute that could end up in court, or if you are reporting suspected corruption.

Written tools are never quick fixes. No matter how brief your points, it takes time and thought to commit them to paper. You can, however, use that time efficiently by planning ways to adapt and reuse everything you write. A letter to an official can become a fact sheet for a personal meeting, or testimony for a public hearing. An email can be the basis for a blog post. Excerpts from your rule-making comments will be welcomed by your trade association; they can also be posted your website. Most importantly, every writing task you tackle will make you a better, faster writer.

Email and Postal Letters

It is a mistake to view email and postal letters as interchangeable. Even if both are appropriate in a given situation, one is likely to be more persuasive than the other, depending on the audience and what you need to communicate.

Because email is so widely used in business, it probably comes naturally to you as a means of communicating with government. Obviously, it maximizes the speed of communication and the ease of replication. Many people who still feel daunted by other types of composition are comfortable with email. In fact, if you are addressing an issue that affects many businesses, like a state regulation, you do not even need to write your own text: The websites of many business organizations offer standardized e-advocacy messages. With no more effort than a few clicks, you can customize the format or deliver it in the original format to a who's-who list of decision makers.

But this very simplicity can undermine an email's persuasiveness. Think about it from an official's point of view: If you were deluged with hundreds, perhaps thousands, of near-identical communications, how closely would you read any one of them?

Depending on the goal of your communication, this may not be a problem. Perhaps you simply want to join a collective advocacy movement on behalf of the whole business community—for example, an effort to show lawmakers that thousands of people are mobilizing for, or against, a new regulation. In this case, it is enough to get counted.

But if you want to make a specific request or get a question answered via email, it is critical to compose your own message. Write with care and precision, just as you would in any other business document; the informality of email does not justify sloppiness. Be scrupulous about using correct names and titles and a professional, respectful tone. Also, provide offline contact information so your identity can be verified.

Odd though it seems in a wired world, postal mail can sometimes be a better choice than email. In general, your hard-copy missive will stand out from the pack—just because relatively few people still take the time to stuff and stamp an envelope. So much advocacy has shifted online that the average mayor who once received 50 constituent letters each week might now be surprised to see 10.

The more specific reason to go postal: if you need to supplement the text with other materials. For example, your complaint about a property maintenance code may not make sense without diagrams and photographs. By including them as part of a neat, well-organized physical package, you will maximize their impact. It may be possible to scan the same documents into an email, but online attachments are easily overlooked, ignored, or deleted.

However, form letters have limited persuasiveness no matter how they are delivered. If you plan to make the extra effort to use postal mail, make it pay off by composing your own message. Keep it succinct, but use the opportunity to show how well you know your subject. Even an official who routinely ignores other types of communication will almost always respond to a thoughtful letter. It may not be the response you sought—but the door will be open for follow-up.

Tips and Techniques

Stay away from colored, textured paper, decorated envelopes, or fancy boxes for your postal materials. It is a waste of money and a sign of inexperience. Never send breakable items or original documents unless there is some critical reason—such as a legal requirement—to do so.

Also, be sure to include your name and (physical) address. In a government office, anonymous packages, no matter how compelling, will be ignored or discarded.

Testimony

The word itself sounds daunting: Because *testimony* is best known as courtroom narrative, some people believe they need legal advice to write it. But as used in the normal course of interactions with government, testimony is nothing more than text you prepare to read, or "testify," at a public meeting. No one expects citizen testimony to be lawyerly; in fact, simple sincerity is more compelling than polished oratory.

Tips and Techniques

Determining when and how you will be allowed to testify to a particular group of officials can be harder than writing the text itself.

Every public body has its own rules: For instance, you cannot assume that a 10-minute narrative will be permitted by the city council just because you presented it to a committee of state legislators.

At a minimum, expect restrictions on how long, on which topics, and at what point in the meeting you can speak. To participate in many public hearings, you must sign up in advance. Research these procedures well in advance (online or by phone) so you do not waste time preparing testimony that never gets heard—or worse, miss an opportunity to speak when your input would make the most difference.

Developing persuasive testimony is not easy. It requires careful research and clear (though not necessarily dramatic) expression. However, it can serve multiple purposes. After reading it as a speech, you can use it again as a background document for personal meetings, a letter to other businesspeople, an op-ed in local newspapers, or a blog post. Unless it is highly specialized, you may be able to adapt the same testimony to several meetings on different topics. For example, if you testified to legislators that a new environmental regulation would hurt your construction business, you could make similar points to county commissioners against an impact fee, or to the mayor about his proposed zoning restrictions.

Whatever the subject of your testimony, remember that it will outlive the proceedings. Like testimony in a court of law, it becomes part of the official record: This means that what you say may be revisited many times and paraphrased in many ways—by officials, allies, opponents, other interested citizens, and the media.

Of course, the heart of effective testimony is a compelling message. The next chapter explains how to craft such a message. But in general, you can boost your impact by observing these dos and don'ts:

Do:
- Identify yourself and your company, including physical location and distinguishing features like number of employees or years in business. If you have some professional certification relevant to the subject or to the group you are addressing, say so. For instance, a legislative health committee would want to know that you are a doctor.
- State precisely what you are supporting or opposing. For example, you may oppose restrictions on home-based businesses but support licensure of some of them.

- Offer concrete, realistic illustrations. How many jobs will you eliminate if a proposed regulation goes into effect? How much are you paying to adhere to the current property maintenance code?
- Make your points in priority order. Chances are, not all of them will be noted or remembered; so try to leave enough time to repeat what you consider most significant.
- Focus on being audible, not on being theatrical.
- Bring enough copies of your testimony and business cards to distribute to every official (and to reporters, if you are seeking media attention).

Don't:
- Get testy if you are challenged, or asked for more information. View it as an opportunity to restate your facts and reemphasize your message.
- Guess the answer to a question. Offer to get back to the questioner (and don't forget!)
- Rely on rhetoric. Calling some policy a "death threat to local business" might get you a headline, but is not conducive to a productive exchange. You will accomplish more by calling the officials' attention to how many stores have closed since the policy began.
- Shout. Use the microphone even if you have a loud voice (some mikes are just for recording, not for amplification).
- Ignore basic rules of courtesy and professionalism. For example, do not exceed the time limit; interrupt or disparage another speaker; tell silly jokes; make off color remarks; or neglect to thank the officials for their attention.

Tips and Techniques

Every speaker has her own style. Still, if you are testifying for the first time, you can get good ideas by listening to veterans. Look on your state's homepage for archived webcasts of public hearings. Your trade association may keep its own recordings or transcripts. Better yet, attend a meeting of the group you wish to address.

Petitions

Fundamentally, all petitions are alike: They are collective demands for action. Around the country, businesspeople have turned to them as a means of getting attention or forcing change. For example, Missouri activists launched a petition drive in 2008 to block the government from taking private property. Soon after Massachusetts increased its sales tax in 2009, citizens began collecting signatures on a proposal to repeal it. However, the use of this tool can be complicated and challenging, depending on what you hope to accomplish.

In 24 states, citizens have the power to place their proposals on a statewide ballot, with or without the support of lawmakers. The two major types of proposals are initiatives (new laws) and referenda (repeal of existing laws). Many local governments offer some form of access to their own ballots, either for municipal initiatives and referenda or for "non-binding" questions (these express the sentiment of the community without affecting laws). But to get there, petitioners must clear some daunting hurdles. Although rules differ by state and jurisdiction, the minimum number of signatures can range into seven figures (the Missouri group collected over 400,000 names—and still fell short). There are strict procedural requirements, like who is eligible to sign and how signatures must be authenticated. Large-scale petition drives are costly—and even if an initiative gets as far as the ballot, there is always the possibility that voters will reject it.

But you can wield a petition effectively, and with much less effort, to achieve goals unrelated to the ballot. Think of it as a marketing device: By circulating a petition, you can call attention to your issue, educate others, and mobilize support. When you deliver a petition to an official or governing body, it shows that your concerns are shared by the community—and that you are serious about getting them addressed. For example, it is one thing to tell the mayor that you are sick of red tape in city offices—and another to present a thousand signatures in support of a streamlined procedure.

How do you begin? For a statutory petition (to obtain ballot access), you must research applicable laws. These are usually available from the board of elections. Otherwise, you have the freedom to design any kind of document you wish, as long as it includes three elements: a heading ("A Petition to Mayor Brown"); a statement of what you support, oppose, or request ("We the undersigned demand a rollback of the commercial license fee"); and lined spaces for signatures and contact information. If you are free of legal constraints, plan to circulate your petition online as well as in person.

Tips and Techniques

Numerous websites offer guidance and support for citizen petitions. Although you may not need the help, it's worth checking a few—like MyPetitionOnline.com and LobbyingForum.com—to get a sense of your options.

Blogging

One increasingly effective way to speak up about an issue is to blog about it. You can get some attention by posting thoughtful comments on the blogs of others (see Section 3 for suggestions). But if you hope to stand out in the marketplace of ideas and opinions, you could consider starting a blog of your own.

Getting a blog up and running is the easy part: Any number of sites, like Blogger and WordPress, offer free, ready-to-use templates. But if you can't do blogging right, there is no reason to do it at all. The challenge is to decide if you have enough time, patience, and motivation to make it worth the effort. Unless you are a celebrity, no one will read your blog with any frequency unless it is interesting and well written. To keep it fresh, you need to commit to posting often and at some reasonable length.

Ask yourself: Exactly how can blogging advance my interests? For example, it would be an excellent vehicle to call attention to a petition drive. A local business blog could educate your community about the impact of statewide policies in their backyard. But you will accomplish nothing by simply railing against bureaucrats or politicians—except make enemies of the officials you complain about. A blog is not a problem-solving or relationship-building device: It is a megaphone.

Another question to consider is whether you are comfortable describing your business problems, or even expressing your opinions, on the Internet. Although you can password-protect your blog to limit the range of people allowed to comment, you can never erase what has been written. Think about how future clients or colleagues might interpret it.

SECTION 2: PERSONAL CONTACT

Written records have distinct advantages, but direct human connections still make a difference. When time is of the essence, a phone call will convey urgency. A personal meeting can bring your issue to life in a way that no document can.

Phone Calls

Some situations demand immediate action. If a key vote is scheduled for this afternoon, you cannot assume the lawmaker will read an email you send this morning. Perhaps you need a fast answer to a question because you're up against a filing deadline. Times like these are when you should pick up a phone.

Don't kid yourself: A single call has limited persuasiveness, whatever the issue. Unless you are able to speak directly to the decision maker, the best you can do is leave a message—which may or may not be accurately conveyed. Still, responsible staff will recognize when the matter is exigent. Also, they keep track of how many calls come in on the same topic, from similar types of people, or requesting a particular response.

Unless you are calling just to ask a simple question or schedule an appointment, two steps will maximize your effectiveness:

1. Rehearse the call in your mind before you make it. Better yet, jot down some notes to make sure you don't forget anything: What is the nature of your problem? Are others involved? Do you need information, or intervention? Most importantly, be clear about what you want this official to do: Contact another department? Vote a certain way? Give you guidance? The more explicit your request, the more constructive (and prompt) the response you're likely to get.
2. Follow up. Nagging never helps, but it is reasonable to call back once a week until someone takes action. If appropriate, ask for the name of the staffperson working on your case, and confirm by email your understanding of who is responsible for what. If you sense that you are being ignored or not taken seriously, do not waste time making accusations: simply call another official.

Personal Meetings

In some situations, a personal meeting is the best—or only—way to get results. For instance, a particular official may be unresponsive to phone calls or emails. To grasp a problem, he might need to see, hear, smell, or taste something. Perhaps you feel more confident in your face-to-face communication skills than in your writing. If the topic is potential corruption, you may not be ready to document your suspicions.

But whether or not it is necessary, a personal meeting is always desirable when it can establish a relationship, ferret out information, or ratchet up an official's level of involvement with your issue. Of course, you must meet with someone who is knowledgeable about the rules and has sufficient authority to make a decision. Remember Lou Paparozzi, the veteran bureaucrat quoted in Chapter One? "I've seen it over and over," he says, "By sitting down with elected officials or higher-level staff instead of just complaining, people get help they otherwise would never have gotten. Not every problem can be solved the way they want, but there is always something to be gained by reaching out—even if it's only understanding how to avoid the same frustration next time."

However, the meeting will not be productive unless you prepare for it. Develop a plan of action: Which points do you intend to cover, and how? What documents and leave-behind materials will you bring? Who (if anyone) should accompany you? What outcome do you seek? In addition to its problem-solving potential, the meeting is an opportunity to impress a powerful person with your savvy, persuasiveness, and determination.

Tips and Techniques

You need not start from scratch to create leave-behind materials. Any letter or testimony you have written on the same topic can be boiled down to a fact sheet or summary document. Most important: Attach your business card!

Especially if you have not met with government officials before, observe these key dos and don'ts:

Do:
- Avoid hubris. You will command respect from public officials by being professional and courteous—not by bragging about your own importance or expressing disdain for their work.
- Make sure you meet with someone who is in a position to help you. For example, there is no point in discussing your regulatory problem with a public affairs assistant.
- Bring one or two other people if they can add an extra dimension to your case, like special expertise or personal experience.
- As soon as possible after the meeting, follow up with an email or letter summarizing your understanding of what was discussed and/or agreed to.

Don't:

- Assume there will be a record of your meeting: Although public meetings are routinely transcribed, personal meetings with public officials are not. It is always appropriate to take notes, or to ask if another person present in the room can do so.
- Squander valuable meeting time by provoking arguments, making baseless accusations, or endlessly repeating your complaints. State your case; provide background information; answer questions; sum up; and stop.
- Bring three or more extra people without asking permission.
- Forget to say thank you.

SECTION 3: COMMUNICATING THROUGH THE MEDIA

Some problems, like burdensome regulation, affect a broad swath of the business community. Others, like corruption, can be counted on to resonate with everyone. Anytime your issue has an impact on many people outside your own firm, there is a potential opportunity to work with the media. Specifically, you can enlist the help of professional journalists in spreading the word.

The huge advantage of this approach: The fans of any established (and at least modestly successful) print or broadcast vehicle will pay attention to a topic just because it gets coverage in that outlet. You automatically get a huge head start over any competing advocate. The disadvantage is that you cannot control how a third party interprets and explains—or fails to explain—your message. For example, if you run a home-building business, you can use your own blog to slam a proposed impact fee as a "housing killer." But despite your best efforts to influence another blogger, he might tout it as a "counterweight to greedy contractors." The potential upside may be worth the risk; but each situation (and media professional) is unique, and you must make a careful judgment.

Assuming you choose this route, it is no less important to research different journalists and vehicles than it is to research government. Unless you have established media relationships, the most direct way to get a reporter's attention is to offer information related to subjects she has written about. It is a waste of time to make random calls to everyone listed on a homepage or masthead: Instead, search archives upfront to learn who has covered stories in your ballpark.

(If there is no archive, or you cannot identify a clear prospect, call an editor or producer to ask.)

Tips and Techniques

Every journalist has his own voice, a characteristic style or perspective that colors how he writes. When reading archived articles, be alert to these nuances. Someone who tends to be hypercritical of business—or simply nasty—would not be your best target.

It is very hard to break into any vehicle with a statewide or national audience. You can try, but it is more efficient to focus on regional or community media (fortunately, these are proliferating online). Although you will have a leg up at any outlet that showcases small business news, the vast majority of local media have some interest in the economy even if they specialize in something else. Also, keep in mind that any vehicle updated daily has a much bigger appetite— and more space—for new information than a weekly or monthly publication.

Like any other cold call, your initial contact with a journalist may or may not produce results. Just as you would with a potential customer, make a pitch for your "product"—in this case, information that you believe will help or interest others. Simply identify yourself and state what you have or can get, without a chatty, long-winded, or jocular introduction. Media professionals work on tight deadlines; they appreciate leads but hate distractions. Also, keep in mind that reporters are trained to be skeptical: If your story is not taken at face value, this is a professional precaution, not a personal slight.

Tips and Techniques

A common knock on journalists is that they are biased. This is true: Their "bias" is for solid, newsworthy information. If all you offer is unsubstantiated rumors—or all you want to do is vent— don't expect to be taken seriously.

On the other hand, once you get a reporter's attention, it is up to you to be clear, precise, and truthful, both in what you say and in how you say it.

Press Releases

If you are uncomfortable cold-calling a journalist—or if that approach doesn't work—you can write a press release. This sounds more challenging than it is. You need no special training to prepare an effective release: Just think of it as another way to organize and emphasize the same facts you would convey in a conversation. The same release can be sent to both print and broadcast media.

A press release need not be lengthy, eloquent, or complicated. But to be effective, it should include these elements: What is the news? Who is involved? Where and when is it happening? Why does it matter? Crucially, it must be accurate and based on thorough research—especially if it is likely to provoke an unfriendly response.

For example, here is a press release about a red tape problem:

For Immediate Release: My Town, Today's Date

Sue Smith, owner of Smith's Appliances, today sent a letter to Mayor Jones calling on him to address the bureaucratic incompetence at city hall. Trying to learn about government-sponsored small business loans, Smith made three separate visits to the Office of Finance and Taxation. Each time, she was told that no one had the right information.

"This shows that our tax dollars are going to waste," said Smith. "If Mayor Jones is concerned about small businesses in My Town, he will replace the know-nothing bureaucrats in that office with competent people."

Smith will appear at next week's city council meeting to present a copy of the letter signed by other local businesspeople. Anyone who wishes to support this effort is encouraged to contact her at smithapplicances.com.

On the face of it, this is a perfectly serviceable release. As long as it is printed (or read on-air) verbatim—as is the practice in some local media—she will have accomplished her goal of calling attention to her problem and putting pressure on Jones to solve it. However, a journalist is under no obligation to accept Smith's version of the story. If you issue a press release with factual flaws or unfounded assertions, here is what can happen to it:

For Immediate Release: My Town, Today's Date

In a letter sent today to Mayor Jones, Sue Smith, owner of Smith's Appliances, accused officials in the Office of Finance and Taxation of "bureaucratic incompetence." According to Smith, OFT staff failed on three occasions to provide her with information about government-sponsored small business loans. She is calling on Jones to replace the individuals.

But Jones responded to the letter by saying that Smith simply went to the wrong office. A centerpiece of his economic growth initiative, Smith stated, is the new Small Business Help Desk in the City Clerk's Department. As described on My Town's website: "The Help Desk is designed to offer comprehensive information on matters that involve different levels of government, like small business loans. Staff are specially trained to access and explain federal, state and county programs. It is open 9–5 at the City Clerk's Department." Jones added: "I am extremely proud of the Help Desk and of all the hardworking public servants at City Hall."

In this example, Smith not only failed to achieve her communication goal—she ended up looking foolish. You can avoid the same mistake by doing your homework before writing a release.

Letters to the Editor or Op-Eds

Another avenue is to write a letter to the editor, or an op-ed (an essay that runs in the opinions and editorials section of a publication). Although this limits your communication to print media, it gives you more control than other approaches.

A letter to the editor is a comment on a story, column, or previous letter. Depending on the publication, typical letters may range in length from as little as 50 words to as many as 250. But most established outlets have limited space and rigid restrictions, so you should check on the letters page for guidelines—and take them seriously. Don't think you can convince someone to make an exception based on the quality of your prose or the urgency of your issue: You can't.. If your letter is too long, an editor will condense it in ways you may not like—or simply reject it.

The best letters are tightly focused on one or two points. They eschew obscure references, metaphors, or jokes. It is important to state upfront why you are writing: To refute an argument? To provide information? Also, if it is relevant, the letter can be used to tell readers what you hope they will do or how they can learn more. Check the model letters in the Appendix for structural guidance.

Tips and Techniques

Reputable publications will not publish a letter to the editor if they cannot verify the identity of the author. Because an email address is usually considered insufficient, do not send in your letter without a phone number and postal address. If you have a good reason for wishing to remain anonymous, call the editor in advance to discuss it.

Because the average op-ed can be three or four times the length of a letter, this format allows you to make a more detailed case. It is particularly effective when your issue is complicated or you are responding to multiple opponents. However, verbosity in itself is not persuasive. As with a letter, it is best to focus on a small number of key points, bolstered with specific (preferably local) examples. If you are refuting an argument, don't just assert that it is wrong; explain why. You can use strong, evocative language in an op-ed, as long as it is grounded in facts and steers clear of vitriol or personal attacks. The model op-ed in the Appendix will help you get started.

Be realistic about the chances of seeing your op-ed in print: State-wide dailies and national outlets receive far more submissions than they can use. But small community-oriented publications are generally open to contributions from local businesspeople. They are also more likely than bigger media to publish your text in its entirety.

Why not bypass editorial control by commenting directly online, using the feedback mechanism on published articles or reporters' blogs? In fact, users of this approach—especially anonymous contributors—now far outnumber those who stick with traditional mechanisms. Unfortunately, these unfettered message boards have created a communications monster. As described by Wall Street Journal columnist L. Gordon Crovitz: "The latest online reality [is] comment sections so uncivilized and uninformative that it's clear the free flow of anonymous comments has become way too much of a good thing. . . . The hope was that people would be civil. Instead, many comment areas have become wastelands of attacks and insults."[2] In response, an increasing number of sites and blogs have begun to filter or edit online comments. Some allow only paying subscribers to comment; others give readers their own screening tool. However the changes evolve, the current free-for-all is unlikely to continue.

Tips and Techniques

If your issue has statewide or national impact, it is certainly worth trying to break into major media outlets. But be careful: Some large publications will not consider a submission that has been offered to their competitors. Check websites for these rules, and to learn how you will be notified when (or if) your op-ed will be published.

Talk Radio

There is a simple reason for the growing popularity of talk radio: In the universe of mass media, it is uniquely accessible to ordinary people. With the exception of a handful of celebrity-oriented shows, the format is, in fact, driven by the interests and opinions of callers. If you are persistent—and well-spoken—you can realistically hope to get time on even a top-rated program.

The challenge of talk radio is not so much how to break in, but how to deal with the host once you are on the air. Even if you are careful to call only business-friendly programs, you can encounter a prickly, combative personality. Remember, all talk show hosts are entertainers. They welcome interesting, well-informed guests, but will not hesitate to play devil's advocate—or worse. Unless you are prepared with facts and reasoned arguments, a few minutes on talk radio could hurt more than help.

If you choose this route, begin by checking station websites for call-in rules specific to each show. Also, take these precautions:

1. You will have very little time to communicate a message. So from the moment you get on the air, stay focused on one or two key points.
2. Regardless of the host's demeanor, don't be defensive. Try not to waste time on jokes and pointless banter.
3. If possible, avoid calling from your car. Not only is it potentially dangerous, but a land connection is usually clearer and more stable.

Tips and Techniques

Before you pick up the phone to call a show on a given day, listen
to other live callers. The host might have chosen that day to showcase a particular point of view or type of problem. His choice
could mean a stronger—or weaker—platform for you.

SECTION 4: APPLICATIONS

Certain communication tools are especially suited to particular problems. In some cases, you must conform to communication requirements or expectations. However, there is always some degree of
flexibility. Tools can be mixed and matched so you can speak up in
whatever way makes you most comfortable—and most persuasive.
Here are a few suggestions:

Problem: Regulation or Red Tape

It is critical to create written documentation of regulatory or red tape
problems. You should keep a journal-like record of names, dates, conversations, and incidents.

This record can serve multiple purposes. You can use it as the basis
for making comments during the administrative rulemaking process—
both in writing and in a public hearing. In some states, when a hearing
is not initially scheduled, you can request one if you feel your plea will
be stronger in person than on paper.

If your problem is caused by a federal rule, your documentation can
also be adapted to the U.S. SBA's "r3" initiative. The program is specifically designed to encourage small business feedback, but you can
only participate by submitting a written evaluation of the rule and recommendations for changing it.

Your "journal" can help you develop an agenda for a personal
meeting, and a summary document to leave with officials who meet
with you. The entries will also give you a head start on emails or letters. Once you have some basic text, it will be easy to communicate
with any decision maker in a position to be helpful. Especially with a
red tape problem, make sure to compile a complete list of departments
and individuals involved in any way. Document each decision maker's decision or action and take it upon yourself to circulate this information among everyone on your list.

It can be productive to communicate with an official even if she has only indirect authority in your case. For example, you should let your state lawmaker know about your problem with a state regulation. It may be an administrative matter—in other words, under the control of a state agency, not the legislature—but she can reach out to agency officials in ways that you cannot.

If you believe that you were treated badly by a municipal department, the mayor should be informed of your experience. In fact, you should consider bringing the matter up during the public comment portion of a city council meeting.

Does your issue affect many people or different communities? If so, there will always be a newspaper, blog, or talk radio host interested in hearing about it.

Note: It is important—and sometimes difficult—to keep your cool and be realistic when communicating about a regulatory or red tape issue. Even when officials are sympathetic, you may be told that because of legal requirements or political roadblocks, the problem can't be fixed quickly enough to help you. If this happens, keep in mind that you have still won a significant victory by setting the wheels in motion for longer-term change—or simply by establishing a relationship with key bureaucrats who can be helpful at other times in other ways.

Problem: Corruption

Again, it is best to start with a written record of what you have seen, heard, or read that strikes you as potentially illegal. Then you can call your community's whistleblower hotline, file a complaint in writing with the ethics commission, or turn over the documentation to appropriate law enforcement authorities.

One surprisingly effective way to head off potential corruption is simply to bring it up at a public meeting. For example, if you call on local officials to enact strong ethics laws in their jurisdiction, it will put them on notice that someone is watching. If you request copies of their financial disclosures, they will know the information is being scrutinized.

Many people are loathe to get involved in what may become a criminal investigation. If you are uncomfortable pursuing a corruption issue personally, another option is to meet with an ethics or law enforcement official who can be trusted to keep the discussion confidential. However, it is still important to keep notes—if only to protect yourself.

Also, consider calling an investigative journalist. A professional reporter can shield his sources if necessary, and you might succeed in launching a major corruption probe without linking your name to it.

KEY POINTS TO REMEMBER

- Written words have staying power—especially when they become part of the public record.
- Direct, face-to-face interactions will add dimension and depth to almost any communication.
- Communicating through the media is a trade-off: You sacrifice some message control in return for wide exposure.
- Even when you must conform to format requirements, communication tools can always be mixed and matched to take advantage of your strengths and preferences.

NOTES

1. Quoted in V. Gray and D. Lowery, "Where Do Policy Ideas Come From? A Study of Minnesota Legislators and Staffers," *Journal of Public Administration Research and Theory* 10, no. 3(2000), 573–97.

2. L. Crovitz, "Is Internet Civility an Oxymoron?" *Wall Street Journal*, April 19, 2010, p. A17.

8

Speak Up II: Message Development

OVERVIEW

However you choose to speak up, your message is what you want officials to hear. It is more than a complaint or a demand. An effective message stands out from other communications because it is focused and purposeful. It gives the listener reasons why he should pay serious attention to you.

Let's say two businesspeople request meetings with the mayor in the hope of altering the property maintenance code. The mayor sees one of them in the morning and the other in the afternoon. Mr. Morning vents about all the money he is losing and threatens to make a big donation to the mayor's political opponent unless there is a change. Mr. Afternoon proposes a way to streamline the code to help businesses while respecting the upkeep standards of the town. Which advocate is more likely to get results?

The daily environment of a government official is a cacophony of often-conflicting communications. The quality of your message will determine whether you break through—or just add to the noise.

Section 1: Setting a Goal

Businesses set goals for sales and profits. When you communicate with government, you also need a clear objective for what you hope to convey and accomplish.

Section 2: Framing Your Message

Framing is the process used to give your message the shape, perspective, and context it needs to stand out.

Section 3: Message Comprehension and Tone

If you are not understood, you cannot be persuasive. And an otherwise compelling message can miss the mark if it is delivered in an inappropriate tone.

Section 4: Choosing a Messenger

Even a successful entrepreneur is not always better off on her own. This section discusses situations where you should consider delivering your message to government through or with others.

* * *

SECTION 1: SETTING A GOAL

An effective message always has a goal. It is as important as the destination for a trip: Without one, the journey has no purpose. Your goal may be short- or long-term; it may be process-oriented (like fighting red tape) or issue-based (like challenging the need for a regulation). It may be focused on achieving reform, or on maintaining the status quo. Whatever its object, as long as it is grounded in fact and conviction, your goal will give direction and clarity to your message.

If goal-setting were easy, every message would be equally purposeful. But that is not the case: Just spend a few hours listening to the daily litany of pleas, demands, and accusations hurled at the average municipal official. Most are long on rhetoric and short on substance. You can provoke some response just by being loud—or emotional—but it is unlikely to be the one you sought.

There are as many goals as there are messages. Still, you will improve your persuasiveness by setting a goal with these characteristics:

1. Specificity

If you plan to testify against a regulation, you will not get far by simply asserting that the regulators are misguided. Agency officials will continue to believe they are acting in the best interests of the community, whether you share that view or not.

Likewise, your testimony will have little value if it is mainly a list of epithets. Instead, think about how you can convey specific, relevant information or experience. Your goal might be to explain the regulation's unintended consequences. Perhaps you can correct inaccuracies, or offer a professional evaluation. Look back at Chapter Two to remind yourself how regulatory impacts differ: Your message should address the specific flaws of one rule, not the general problem of regulation.

2. Realistically related to what officials can do

Even the U.S. president has limited powers. No state or local official can single-handedly accomplish broad, sweeping reforms like restructuring government or improving the competitiveness of the marketplace.

However, every public official has influence within the sphere of his responsibilities and expertise. It is up to you to learn what a specific person (and public body) can and cannot do, and to express your goal accordingly. For example, a state legislator cannot change a federal regulation. A town council cannot build a county road. Of course, there is nothing wrong with presenting a wish list—but wishes rarely come true.

3. Not personal

Even if you are raising questions about potential wrongdoing by an individual, your goal is to stop corruption—not to persecute the individual. You may believe that a certain employee is the biggest impediment to efficiency in city hall, but you will accomplish more by calling attention to the poor service than by bad-mouthing the official. You always have the right (and sometimes, the justification) to assert that someone needs to be fired; but the reality in government is that inefficiency, like other problems, almost always involves more than a single culprit.

4. Not confused with business goals

If you simply regale a government official with tales of woe—how your revenues are falling and your competitors are cheating—do not expect more than sympathy. It is not her job to boost your profits. However, you should certainly cite your problems if they illustrate a broader issue or are affecting other businesses in the jurisdiction.

Realistically, some goals are harder to achieve than others. For example, you can aim at convincing a lawmaker to cast a particular vote. But it is impractical to try changing her overall ideology. By all means, be ambitious—but don't be naive.

SECTION 2: FRAMING YOUR MESSAGE

When you frame a picture, you enhance its visual effect. When you frame a message, you enhance its meaning to your audience. More generally, a message frame is a context. It helps a listener understand how your goal aligns with his.

Of course, you may need to interact with many officials, and you can't know the personal goals of each one. But the vast majority share a broad, community service perspective. They hope to maximize the public good —or at least to maximize the public's satisfaction with their performance.

Let's say you want to change an existing environmental rule. Simply calling for "reform" will not get more than polite nods from rule makers. A more compelling message would tap into the officials' own motivation: to get the best environmental results at the least cost. It would encourage them to see you more as an ally than an adversary. For example, you could frame your suggestions as ways to help the environmental agency:

– Clarify ambiguous language.
– Streamline compliance procedures.
– Eliminate redundant or counterproductive requirements.
– Reduce paperwork.
– Facilitate better environmental protection.

Perhaps your town's current commercial zoning rules depress the resale value of your property. No matter how bitterly you complain at town council meetings, they will not respond just to help you make more money.

But they might consider a new zoning initiative if you show how it would further their goal of attracting new investment. You could point out, for example, that simplifying the waiver process would encourage growing firms to expand in place, instead of moving elsewhere. Relaxing some density or height restrictions could jumpstart new construction. Whatever the situation, here is the key to persuasiveness: Convince the decision maker that it will help him to help you.

The more you know about particular officials or public bodies, the easier it is to frame your message in accordance with their interests and priorities. For example, before presenting testimony to the environmental agency, revisit your research: Have these regulators been receptive to rule modifications in the past? For what reasons? Did you talk informally to agency staff about what ideas have the best chance to be considered?

Before addressing the town council, familiarize yourself with any recent decisions related to commercial zoning. If they tightened restrictions only last month, for instance, it is unrealistic to expect an immediate about-face. However, the timing is perfect to ask the council to monitor the impact of their latest initiative on small business.

Are you meeting with a legislator or mayor? Review her voting record and any public statements relevant to your problem. In particular, try to identify her "signature" issues, those she has worked hardest on and feels passionately about. Is she known as a corruption buster? Then she will be open to your suspicions about shady development deals. Has she supported impact fees? You might want to go elsewhere to seek regulatory relief for builders.

When dealing with any elected official (or a high-profile appointed official, like a state agency commissioner), keep in mind that he is concerned about his public image even if he has limited interest in your issue per se. It will always be helpful to frame your message as a broad-based community concern, and to make him aware that many businesspeople are watching how he votes or what he does.

Sometimes you can choose whether to frame your message positively or negatively. A positive frame means describing what you seek as a gain; a negative frame depicts it as averting a loss. Conventional wisdom suggests that it is always best to be upbeat, a belief bolstered by some consumer research. For instance, one study found that beef buyers were more likely to choose a product when it was labeled "75 percent lean" instead of "25 percent fat."[1]

But overall, the evidence is mixed. And every official—like every issue—is different. Most bureaucrats are risk-averse: They are rarely willing to experiment with a new procedure unless you can prove serious flaws in the current one. However, another official may be bold or entrepreneurial by nature. She might be more enthusiastic about your proposal to change the building code if you present it as a way to encourage innovative architecture, instead of as an impediment to expansion.

Tips and Techniques

You can frame virtually any message either positively or negatively, but it takes practice. As an exercise, try framing your issue both ways. Here are examples to help you get started.

MESSAGE RELATED TO RED TAPE

Positive frame: Businesses can operate more efficiently without it.
  Negative frame: It is discouraging job creation.

MESSAGE RELATED TO REGULATION

Positive frame: Our state would attract more investment without it.
  Negative frame: If it is not changed, businesses will move to
other states.

MESSAGE RELATED TO CORRUPTION

Positive frame: Honest companies thrive in an ethical environment.
  Negative frame: No one wants to do business with crooks.

Another facet of framing is to anticipate opposition. Although you cannot foresee every potential opponent, it is important to keep in mind that in government, a small action can provoke an outsize reaction. For example, your proposal to loosen commercial zoning restrictions could be met with outrage from anti-development activists. Even a seemingly innocuous change, like reducing red tape for new restaurants, might raise the ire of public health advocates. You may think that no one would fight a cut in taxes or fees—until there are protests from groups that benefit from that stream of income.

This is not to suggest that you should hold off or back down just because there is pushback. But you must be realistic: Prepare to respond to attacks. Although you might not care what others think, any government official—elected or not—is obligated to listen to both sides of every issue.

In some situations, like a public hearing, you can respond to critics directly. Look for opportunities to question their evidence, experience, inferences, or assumptions, such as:

- On what data are you basing that comment?
- How many times did you have that experience?
- Did you consider alternative plausible conclusions?
- Why did you make those assumptions?

If you cannot respond in person, try to anticipate likely challenges. Provide officials with answers to the questions they are most likely to be asked, and make yourself readily available as a resource should they need additional information.

Tips and Techniques

Don't risk getting blindsided by criticism you didn't expect. If your issue is at all contentious, use your media archive research to pinpoint the most likely points of attack. Also seek advice from your trade association or from others in the community who have taken on similar issues.

SECTION 3: MESSAGE COMPREHENSION AND TONE

Even the most carefully framed message will not be persuasive unless it is comprehended, or understood, by the recipient. You might think that your problem is self-evident, simply because you face it every day; but to your listener it may be meaningless.

Government officials face a daily barrage of messages. Many contain information that is new and complex. To make sense of this bewildering overload, they try to categorize and evaluate it.

It is always easier to understand an unfamiliar concept if you can fit it into a familiar mental framework. That's why the first car was described as a "horseless carriage," and digital representations of text were introduced as "e-books." You can use the same technique to make your issue easier to comprehend. For example, instead of explaining all the onerous record-keeping you do to comply with a local regulation—which could sound like whining to someone who doesn't know your business—you could say: "This regulation generates more paperwork than all the state rules combined." That description (assuming it is accurate) will get the attention of any experienced regulator.

You can also facilitate the evaluation of your issue by referring to simple benchmarks. A $100 fee may not sound like much to a listener who has no basis for comparison. But it takes on a different meaning if you can compare it to the $10 fee charged by a neighboring town for the same service.

Comprehension can be heightened—or undermined—by language. Just as you are stymied by government-speak, others can be confused by techno-jargon or acronyms specific to your business. It takes more time to spell out words than to use abbreviations, and it might bolster your self-confidence to throw around technical terms. But you are hurting your case if your listener can't follow your argument.

Tips and Techniques

Try this simple structural device to get past any initial confusion: Start sentences and paragraphs with familiar terms and information, and then introduce new information at the end. Use concrete examples to illustrate abstract concepts.

Sometimes you can improve comprehension by choosing a particular communication tool: Certain types of information are better understood when conveyed in written form than when transmitted verbally or via audiovisual vehicles. In particular, written tools (by themselves or used together with other tools) can boost comprehension if your message is complicated or runs counter to conventional wisdom.

A message that is clearly understood can still be compromised by an inappropriate tone, or manner of expression. Remember that the way you come across is as crucial as what you say.

Here are dos and don'ts for setting the tone of your message.

Do:

- Be respectful toward government in general, regardless of how strongly you oppose a policy in particular. Trashing bureaucrats and politicians might make you feel good, but it is sure to alienate your listener.

If you doubt the significance of civility, consider the view of Jim Leach, former congressman and chair of the National Endowment for the Humanities:

> Little is more important . . . than establishing an ethos of thoughtfulness in the public square. Words . . . clarify—or cloud—thought and energize action. . . . The concept of civility implies politeness, but civil discourse is about more than good etiquette. At its core, civility requires respectful engagement: a willingness to consider other views and place them in the context of history. . . . If we can't respect our neighbors, how can we expect others to respect us, our values and way of life?[2]

- In a personal interaction, build your case gradually and answer every question patiently. If you are in too much of a hurry, reschedule the meeting.
- In a written message, choose conciliatory language over inflammatory rhetoric. Putting an official on the defensive can be counterproductive—and once your attack is in writing, you can't take it back.

Don't:

- Be a show-off. It is fine to take pride in your accomplishments, but persistently blowing your own horn is obnoxious.
- Use sarcasm or jokes. Government is a serious enterprise; even if you have an established and comfortable relationship with an official, excessive humor is inappropriate.
- Exaggerate or distort information. Any kind of misrepresentation is sure to be exposed, and will permanently destroy your credibility.

Tips and Techniques

To reinforce your appreciation for the impact of tone, consider these two letters to a mayor. The topic and the facts are the same, but one approach comes across as professional and cooperative, while the other is simply hostile.

LETTER #1

I am writing to call your attention to the unintended impact of your recent ban on downtown street parking. By forcing our potential customers to hunt for lots, the new restrictions are hurting Main Street businesses.

I know your goal is to improve pedestrian safety, but the change has actually made them less, not more safe. Drivers are stopping in the middle of Main Street to drop off or pick up shoppers, endangering walkers who cross in front or in back of them.

I share your concerns about safety, but I believe this is the wrong approach. I look forward to meeting with you as soon as possible to discuss alternatives.

LETTER #2

What is the matter with you people at city hall? We business owners pay your salaries, and all you do is punish us!

Your new parking ban is killing our businesses. It is not making people safer. In fact, it is putting pedestrians in more danger than before. Someone is sure to get hurt by a car stopping in the middle of Main Street to drop off or pick up shoppers.

I demand to meet with you and I want to know how soon you intend to change this ridiculous policy.

SECTION 4: CHOOSING YOUR MESSENGER

You can handle many government problems yourself. But sometimes it is necessary—and smart—to speak through or with others, both in personal meetings and for public communication efforts. In a face-to-face dialogue with an official, an ally can reinforce your comments by citing his own experience. If your issue has broad community implications, using multiple spokespeople is a concrete way to demonstrate that breadth.

But to further your effort, any messenger must have credibility—in itself a composite of other characteristics. A credible person is knowledgeable, trustworthy, and likeable. Although she may not be equally strong on all three dimensions, she cannot be persuasive if entirely lacking on any of them. Think about your everyday advisors, the people you turn to for business or personal counsel. You value your lawyer, for example, primarily for his professional expertise; but would you consult an attorney you didn't trust? When you need advice on parenting matters, you ask a friend; but you would find someone else if she knew nothing about children.

A person's level of knowledge can be measured objectively. If it cannot be established on the basis of a certification or degree, knowledge can be reasonably inferred from years of experience or success in a field.

But likeability and trustworthiness are subjective characteristics. This means they are subject to interpretation and cannot be quantified. Psychologists have invented scales that purport to compare people on these dimensions; but for all practical purposes, the only meaningful gauges are your own judgment and a person's reputation.

If someone is widely respected in the community, does that automatically make him an ideal messenger? Unfortunately, no. He may be an excellent doctor, for example, but a poor communicator. A well-known local philanthropist may get an appointment with the mayor sooner than you could get one yourself, but if she is unfamiliar with or unenthusiastic about your issue, including her in the meeting won't help.

On the other hand, it can be extremely valuable to show support from someone considered an "opinion leader" in a field related to your issue—an individual whose expertise and integrity are unassailable. For instance, a top hospital executive could speak very convincingly about a public health regulation. A professor of ethics would be effective in addressing corruption. Whomever you consider tapping to help deliver your message, be certain he understands your goal and is comfortable representing your interests.

Tips and Techniques

When choosing a messenger, watch out for potential conflicts of interest. For example, you would not want someone to speak before the city council on your behalf if that person is suing the municipality. Likewise, it would not be smart to come to a meeting with a lawmaker accompanied by a political candidate who is running against her.

Inviting someone to take part in a personal meeting is straightforward and requires no long-term commitment, on either your part or theirs. However, you bear sole responsibility for ensuring the person is:

- conversant with the topic,
- apprised and fully supportive of whatever you intend to request, and
- on time for the meeting.

If at all possible, you should rehearse your respective roles and agree in advance on answers to the likeliest questions. At a minimum, provide your invitee with copies of key background documents and talking points—and don't wait to share these materials until you are walking into the meeting.

Recruiting others (outside of your immediate circle) to be part of public advocacy—a petition drive, a regulatory hearing, a media push—is more challenging. The stakes can be higher, too: depending on the issue, your chances for success could hinge on demonstrating broad community support. So how do you go about this effort?

The easiest place to begin is with organizations you belong to, especially business or trade groups. If they are not already involved with your issue, ask yourself why. Sometimes the reason will be obvious: A chamber of commerce cannot take a position that would benefit one category of members, like franchises, over another category, like independent stores. In other situations, it is a resource issue: A statewide trade group does not have the time or funds to get involved with local matters. Also, there are restrictions on what a nonprofit organization can do without jeopardizing its legal (and federal tax) status.

Whatever the obstacles, if your existing network can't help, you will need to create a coalition of new supporters. Here are the steps to take:

1. Define your issue as broadly and inclusively as possible.

Remember the old adage "Politics makes strange bedfellows"? So does advocacy: Some of the most unlikely coalitions can also be the most successful.

Let's say you are fed up with red tape and bureaucratic snafus in several of your city's permit and licensing departments. Looking at the problem narrowly, it only affects businesses.

But from a broader perspective, it could also be about top-heavy government (too many bureaucrats with redundant responsibilities); misdirected spending (multiple offices at different sites when one would do); or insufficient transparency (more information could be available online). Each of these issues has its own phalanx of interest groups and advocacy organizations whose efforts could complement yours.

Opponents of public corruption, in particular, have a long history of working with other advocates who might otherwise be at odds over policy and politics. Their motives may be different: In a push to tighten pay-to-play laws, for example, good government groups have long-term policy concerns while businesses want a fair shot at public contracts. But their goal—honesty in government—is the same.

Make a list of potential coalition partners. Do you have a relationship, or even a nodding acquaintanceship, with any of their leaders? If not, reach out to the president or chairperson and request an opportunity to address their membership.

2. Expect to do the lion's share of the work.

The priorities of another group are unlikely to mirror yours. Even if they are bursting with enthusiasm about your effort, do not expect them to divert significant resources from their own mission. Never pressure coalition partners for support they cannot or will not provide. Instead, think about ways to help them help you. For example:

- Education about your issue:
    At a minimum, provide the results of your research and resources for more information.
- Ready-made communications:
    Some organizations prefer to generate their own letters, testimony, and other material. But others will appreciate draft text or talking points.
- Publicity:
    Assuming they are interested, make sure your coalition partners have opportunities to share in your (positive) media exposure.
- Reciprocal support
    It is simple courtesy—as well as good business—to do your best to support the people who support you. Realistically, this will not always be possible. But even when you can't help them, you can usually refrain from hurting them.

Let's say you recently convinced the city council to allow taller buildings in a commercial zone. You got support from a civic group working to preserve open space by encouraging builders to add height instead of width.

Shortly thereafter, the same civic group backs a tourist tax that is strongly opposed by the business community. You cannot support their position. But you can, at least, lay low during the battle. Even if you publicly disagree with them, you can do it diplomatically.

3. Identify both existing and potential opponents.

The more you know about organizations likely to oppose you, the better you will be prepared to fight back. Using the same research techniques you have already learned, look for public statements, position papers, and media reports. Also educate yourself about their funding sources and membership base.

Of course, no matter how diligent your preparation, new opponents can materialize anytime. Old ones could develop new lines of attack. Never get complacent. That doesn't mean you should be paranoid, but you must stay alert.

Tips and Techniques

Because they are experienced in grassroots organizing, partisan political organizations can be valuable coalition partners. But be cautious. Depending on the political climate (and whether an election is imminent), you might risk alienating key officials or nonpartisan interest groups.

KEY POINTS TO REMEMBER

- Your communication goal should be specific, realistic, impersonal, and distinct from your business objectives.
- The single most important key to persuasiveness is to convince a decision maker that it will help him to help you.
- Remember that what you say can be powerfully affected by how you say it.
- Even if you are a successful entrepreneur, the go-it-alone approach is not always best for communicating with government.

NOTES

1. I. Levin and G. Gaeth, "How Consumers are Affected by the Framing of Attribute Information Before and After Consuming the Product," *Journal of Consumer Research* 15 (Dec. 1988), 374–78.

2. J. Leach, "Civil Discourse," *St. Petersburg Times* January 15, 2010, www.tampabay.com.

Conclusion

Reform Rising

For decades, government efforts to cut red tape, curtail regulation, and stem corruption were little more than exotic experiments. Today, these are mainstream initiatives in hundreds of municipalities, counties, and states. In large part, this culture change has been spurred by outspoken businesspeople like you. At the same time, declining tax revenues have forced local officials to acknowledge their own mistakes—or at least, to admit they can do better.

Technology is a significant driver of reform. The steady shift of government communications and operations online is eliminating bureaucratic gatekeepers, streamlining record-keeping, and facilitating citizen education. With e-access to administrative rule making, small businesses can be as forceful as large corporations in shaping new regulations. Around-the-clock access and online support are reducing the headaches and inconvenience of regulatory compliance. Online disclosure of voting, public purchasing, and political fund-raising records leave corrupt officials with few places to hide.

But technology is no panacea. Virtual red tape can be as irritating as the terrestrial kind. Ease of compliance does not lighten the regulatory load. And disclosure, in itself, cannot stop thievery.

Moreover, there are limits to what is practical on a large scale in cyber-government. Take the promising new technology called *enterprise social networking*, an interactive communications portal and information management system customized for the needs of local government. Here is how it is being used in the town of Cary, North Carolina:

> This focused social network (or online community) serves as a one-stop communication tool with the planning department for Cary citizens concerned with town zoning. Through citizen feedback to one portal,

town officials are able to manage and respond quickly and effectively. These responses are then published on the Web site to serve as a reference for residents, preventing the repetition of questions that planning department officials have already answered. This streamlined communication results in an increased response rate and enables officials to devote more time to constituents.[1]

Hopefully, this is a glimpse of the future. But for now, few communities can afford to invest in this type of e-innovation. Also, Cary's population is far more tech-savvy than the average: Reflecting its location in the famous Research Triangle of Raleigh-Durham, 94 percent of residents have Internet access, and high numbers take advantage of web-based public forums. Elsewhere, it can take considerable time (and educational resources) to bring citizens up to speed with cutting-edge applications.

As more and more public business is transacted online, another issue is emerging: Vast quantities of personal data are now routinely digitized and accessible to anyone for any purpose, legitimate or otherwise. Of course, many personal documents, like property deeds and court records, have long been in the public domain. But in the past, it took at least a modicum of effort to retrieve them. Today, an experienced cyber-sleuth (or potential identity thief) can find Social Security numbers, signature images, tax returns, and other sensitive material in a matter of minutes.

Local officials are increasingly aware of the problem, and many are taking steps to redact or obscure certain categories of online information, but there are no uniform standards or privacy-protection requirements. The band-aid approach, although better than nothing, is clearly insufficient. As one Internet law expert observed: "The solution is for all the counties to do it, for all the states to do it . . . [but] you can't take a system in place for more than 100 years and expect it to be fixed overnight."[2]

Fortunately, no one is waiting for technology to eliminate mindless regulation, political corruption, or red tape. Instead, state and local governments around the country have launched promising initiatives to attack each of these problems head-on.

REGULATORY FLEXIBILITY

In 1996, the Small Business Regulatory Enforcement Fairness Act mandated that federal agencies consider the impact of their rules on small firms. Importantly, the new requirement was proactive, making agencies responsible for reaching out to affected businesses instead of waiting for reaction to proposed rules. According to the U.S. SBA, by 2004 these efforts had saved small companies $17.1 billion in averted federal regulatory costs.[3]

However, as discussed in Chapter Two, small businesses also bear a disproportionate regulatory burden at the state and local levels of government, which are not subject to the federal law. In 2002, the SBA drafted model legislation for the states based on the federal review and outreach requirements. By 2009, 44 states had enacted or introduced at least a partial form of regulatory flexibility. There is a clear trend in the right direction.

The SBA recommends five requirements in state laws to give small firms the strongest possible voice in rule making. These elements include:

- A clear "small business" definition
- Analysis of a proposed regulation's economic impact on small business
- Consideration of alternatives less burdensome to small business
- Periodic evaluation of existing regulations
- Judicial review of agency compliance with the regulatory flexibility law

Not every state has adopted all five provisions, but even imperfect laws have opened doors once closed to all but the largest corporations. Moreover, evidence is mounting that regulatory flexibility is a significant economic development tool, motivating both legislators and regulators to improve on current practices.

For example, Massachusetts was a relative latecomer to the legislative scene; as of 2009, the state did not require agencies to analyze the economic impact of regulations on small business. But according to an SBA report, the Department of Public Health "decided to do so as a matter of good government." Here are the results:

Under the Massachusetts Food Protection Program, within the state Department of Public Health, businesses transporting frozen and/or refrigerated products are required to purchase or lease a mechanically refrigerated vehicle. MDPH conducted hearings on updating their frozen dessert regulations and ... small businesses used the opportunity to voice concerns about the adverse impact of the rule on their businesses. As a result of the hearing MDPH revised the regulations to allow any person wanting to use their own method for transporting frozen or refrigerated products to apply for a variance so long as the person could explain how safe temperatures would be maintained.[4]

Without this commonsense change, small firms would have been forced to spend approximately $50,000 to buy a refrigerated truck and several thousands of dollars per year in insurance and operating costs.

Some regulatory flexibility initiatives sound like minor modifications but have produced major benefits. For example, several states have implemented an email regulatory alert system. Simply by reaching out to small businesses who might otherwise be unaware of pending regulation, these states have significantly improved communication, education, access—and goodwill.

More broadly, the vast majority of legislators have come to realize that small businesses are their states' most important engines of growth, job creation, and economic diversification. The recent wave of regulatory flexibility laws shows no sign of receding.

ETHICS REFORM

Governments cannot legislate honesty. But they can set ethical standards; create oversight mechanisms; and mete out harsh punishment to those who cheat, deceive, or rob the taxpayers. Can these measures head off marquee crooks, like the denizens of the "Rogues' Gallery" in Chapter Four? Probably not. But as one prominent ethicist points out, they can "guide the incorruptible and help deter the corruptible."[5] Simply by calling attention to the potential for abuse, ethics laws also encourage public scrutiny—the single most powerful weapon in a democracy's corruption-busting arsenal.

The last decade has seen a steady stream of state and local government ethics reform. As any local newspaper reader knows, some problems remain acute. But others are being averted—or at least ameliorated—by conflict-of-interest regulations, gift restrictions, nepotism bans, and campaign finance rules.

Conflicts of Interest

Even the most reform-minded government cannot eliminate all conflicts of interest, which occur in an infinite variety of settings and forms. Instead, ethics laws define the most common conflicts and tell officials how they must deal with them. This approach is not perfect, but it helps create a culture of vigilance.

For example, dual office-holding—the practice of holding two elected offices at the same time—is generally recognized as a wellspring of dubious decision making. Which master is being served at what time? When interests clash, whose win out? The vast majority of states now ban state lawmakers from holding other statewide offices. About half prohibit legislators from holding county or municipal offices. Where dual office-holding is still allowed, there are restrictions on what a wearer of two hats can earn or do.

Double-dipping, the practice of drawing two government paychecks, is banned or restricted in about half the states. There are also limits on state officeholders seeking government contracts, lobbying on behalf of private interests and representing private clients before public bodies.

Most states now require legislators to file annual personal financial disclosure statements. This is a passive but useful tool to discourage conflicts of interest by telling the public which lawmakers are on whose payroll. These statements typically identify the officeholder's employer, other sources of income, businesses in which he holds an interest, and addresses of any property he owns.

At the local level, conflicts of interest are being addressed in codes of ethics and moonlighting rules. For example, the Code of Ethics of Lumpkin County, Georgia, includes this provision:

> In order to assure independence and impartiality on behalf of Lumpkin County citizens, officials shall not use public positions to influence or otherwise affect government decisions or actions in which they possess a material financial interest. . . . Officials shall disclose investments, interest in real property, and sources of income. . . . Officials shall abstain from participation in deliberations or decision-making where any conflicts are deemed to exist.

The town of Old Orchard Beach, Maine, reminds its employees that they may not "advocate in any public meeting or private discussion any matter in which [they] have a personal or financial interest except upon full and timely disclosure of the interest."

New York City officials are prohibited from holding "a job with anyone that they know or should know does business with the City or that receives a license, permit, grant or benefit from the City."

Of course, such admonitions are only meaningful when they have teeth. Improving the enforcement of conflict-of-interest laws is an ongoing task for ethics reformers.

Gifts

Restrictions on gift-giving and receiving in the public sector are wildly inconsistent across states and local governments. This reflects the general lack of agreement on which, if any, such rules are effective antidotes to corruption. In fact, no one knows if a crime is prevented because a city vendor cannot buy Mayor Smith a Big Mac. But the burger really isn't the point. There is increasingly widespread consensus that gift restrictions can, at a minimum, reassure the public that officials are not for sale.

Most states do not ban all gifts, but only those that exceed some specified value. In general, gifts to legislators from professional lobbyists are subject to the tightest controls, but some rules extend beyond the statehouse to apply to all public officials. The diversity of statutory gift restrictions is illustrated by these examples:

Georgia: Limits the value of permissible gifts to $101.
Michigan: Prohibits gifts exceeding $25 in any one-month period.
Pennsylvania: Bans "anything which is received without consideration of equal or greater value."
Utah: Bans gifts only to employees of the executive branch of state government.

Municipal policies also vary considerably. New York City's rule is simple: No employee can accept anything with a value over $50 from a person or firm doing business with the city. But in San Diego, the restriction applicable to an official depends on that official's responsibilities and scope of authority. Those decision makers deemed "high level" are limited to $420 worth of gifts per year from a single source; "local code" staff are held to a lower standard.

Gift policies in many smaller towns and counties are ineffective, confusing, toothless—or nonexistent. A survey of local governments in Connecticut, for example, found that 46 percent have no restrictions at all.[6] However, there is increasing pressure from civic groups around the country to impose some meaningful controls.

Nepotism

Nepotism policies, especially in local government, have proven thorny and hard to enforce. If Alderman Jones wants to circumvent a ban in Ethics City, he can make a deal with his friend in a neighboring town: You hire my son, I'll hire yours. State Senator Smith can quietly but firmly ask a state-regulated company (or a nonprofit dependent on state grants) to employ his wife. Efforts to tighten the rules are typically countered with some version of the argument made by one town councilman in Connecticut: " 'I can't support something that is so restrictive because it would discriminate against qualified people just because they happen to be relatives of certain town officials.' "[7]

Still, nearly half the states prohibit lawmakers from hiring their relatives. And whether or not it is restricted by law, nepotism has become politically toxic. Especially when local budgets are tight, nothing triggers the fury of voters like charges that someone was hired because of her family connections.

Campaign Finance

A briefing paper on campaign finance reform published by the National Conference of State Legislatures sets the stage with this anecdote:

> In early 2009, Apple approved sales of an iPhone application, "Pay2-Play," a game where users, acting as governor, must raise funds by buying and selling senate seats and government jobs to remain in office. The game—amusing to some and offensive to others—highlights the attention paid to an ethics and campaign finance issue that has been percolating in the states.[8]

The problem is pay-to-play: the practice of giving money or other benefits to public officials in return for jobs, contracts, votes, favors, or privileges. The issue is how to stop it without undermining free speech.

Caps on how much a donor can give to a political candidate are widespread. Although the rules are inconsistent, by 2011 there will be only four states with no limits at all. It is also common to restrict contributions to political action committees and party organizations. But tying limits to procurement is a relatively new approach; eight states currently ban certain gaming contractors from making political donations, while nine states apply pay-to-play restrictions to a broad range of existing and prospective public vendors. Most of the more comprehensive state laws apply in some way to candidates and officials at other levels of government: for example, a school board candidate cannot take money from a purveyor of playground equipment to the school.

At both the state and local levels, pay-to-play rules are frequently challenged in the courts. Businesses complain that the laws impinge on their rights. Politicians chafe at the complex, confusing disclosure requirements. However, the trend toward tighter and more sweeping restrictions is unlikely to be reversed—at least until public corruption recedes from the headlines.

RED TAPE REVIEW

To a greater extent than the other initiatives, red tape reviews are bubbling up from city halls instead of starting at the statehouse. That makes sense, as local officials are on the front line of what citizens perceive as a war on wasteful requirements. They are also spurred by the need to cut budgets and attract new investment, as municipal and county revenue streams get hammered by a nationwide recession.

Local governments are finding ways to speed up permitting processes, streamline licensure applications, and give small businesspeople other opportunities to track and expedite the status of their paperwork. For example, more than a dozen Massachusetts towns cut their permitting times from over two years to a matter of months, a key issue for high-tech companies seeking to expand in the region.[9] As discussed in Chapter Five, many municipalities are consolidating their small business services into one-stop shops.

Los Angeles cut red tape as a way to save its signature industry: In 2008, feature film production was in a tailspin because location managers were stymied by a bewildering bureaucracy. Multiple departments had authority over everything from when filming could start to what the crew could eat for lunch, but no one at city hall was empowered to troubleshoot on behalf of the managers. After the mayor appointed "film liaisons" in every department, movie-making significantly rebounded.[10]

In New York City, where over 3,000 new restaurants open each year, a 2010 pilot program called the New Business Acceleration Team took aim at the bureaucratic obstacles faced by these fledging eateries. By stressing coordination and cross-training among city agencies, the approach quickly succeeded in shaving weeks—even months—off the average time necessary to complete inspections and permits.[11]

New Jersey's Red Tape Review Group led a state-level assault on red tape. Led by the lieutenant governor, the panel issued a scathing 130-page report calling for the elimination of many regulations and over 120 public bodies. As Lieutenant Governor Kim Guadagno commented: "From some bureaucrat sitting in Trenton [the state capitol], we've created a whole arm of government that's gotten out of hand. . . . We have milk police, we have parking police, we have wine-tasting police, we have tire police. These are the kinds of things that make it nearly impossible for businesses."[12]

So on each of these fronts, reform is rising. State and local governments are increasingly comprehensible, accessible, and responsive to small business. But there is no guarantee that progress will continue. The future depends on people like you staying alert and involved in your community.

Realistically, there are limits to what these reforms can accomplish. Even the most far-reaching and well-meaning new policies will never completely eliminate mindless regulation, corruption, or red tape. But by using the tools you have learned in this book, you can effectively fight back. You may still get some grief, but you'll also get access and opportunities. And you will know that you've made a difference—the most important achievement of all.

KEY POINTS TO REMEMBER

- E-government initiatives, although not panaceas, are substantially improving small business access to state and local government.
- Regulatory flexibility laws are opening doors to the administrative rule-making process and to other opportunities once closed to all but the largest corporations.
- Ethics reforms cannot stop corruption, but they are important tools to "guide the incorruptible and help deter the corruptible."[13]
- Red tape reviews are bubbling up from the grassroots as officials at all levels seek to boost local business and attract new investment.
- To ensure continued progress, it is critical for you to stay alert and involved in your community!

NOTES

1. D. Bevarly and J. Ulma, "Citizen Involvement in the Digital Age," *The Public Manager.org*, June 13, 2008.

2. M. McCreary as quoted in J. Fry, "When Public Records are Too Public," *Wall Street Journal*, June 25, 2007, www.wsj.com.

3. SBA Office of Advocacy, "Regulatory Flexibility: What It is and Why It Matters," State Guide to Regulatory Flexibility for Small Businesses, 2007, *www.sba.gov/advo*.

4. SBA Office of Advocacy, "Lizzy's Ice Cream Parlor: A Case for Common Sense Regulation," State Regulatory Flexibility Model Legislative Initiative 2009 Legislative Activity, 2009, www.sba.gov/advo.

5. M. Davies, "Addressing Municipal Ethics: Adopting Local Ethics Laws," in *Ethics in Government*, 108 (New York Bar Association, Albany: NY, 2002.

6. Common Cause Connecticut, "2004 Municipal Ethics Survey," 2005, www.commoncause.org.

7. As quoted in Weizel, R. (2008), "Stratford Official Attacks Nepotism," Connecticut Post May 12, www.ctpost.com.

8. N. O'Donnell Wood, "Pay-to-Play: State Reforms," National Conference of State Legislators Legisbrief 17, no. 28, (2009), www.ncsl.org.

9. R. Weisman, "Towns That Cut Red Tape Score High," Boston Globe, November 26, 2007, www.boston.com.

10. P. Willon, "LA City Council Lists Top 10 Places Where Bureaucracy Makes It Hard to Film," *Los Angeles Times*, November 18, 2009, www.latimes.com.

11. M. H. Saul, "One-Stop Shop for New Businesses," *Wall Street Journal* May 22–23, 2010, p. A18.

12. L. Kwoh, and L. Fleisher "NJ Lieutenant Governor's Report Recommends Cutting Red Tape for Businesses," Star Ledger April 19, 2010, www.starledger.com.

13. Davies, "Addressing Municipal Ethics: Adopting Local Ethics Laws."

Appendix

Models
Glossary

Models

Letter #1: Supporting a position

Dear Editor:

Thank you for your editorial endorsing flexible height restrictions for new commercial construction in Pleasant Town. Your recent stories on this topic have been very informative.

I would also like to point out to readers that by allowing some builders to add height instead of depth, we can preserve green space on city streets. This will benefit citizens who want attractive, open urban streetscapes as well as businesses desiring to expand in place.

Other towns that have instituted flexible restrictions report increased occupancy rates and higher rents in downtown districts. This data is available on the chamber of commerce website, www.pleasanttownchamber.com. I hope readers will join me in urging the mayor to support this change in the zoning code as an economic development tool for our community.

Fred Smith
Smith Realty
1 First Street, Pleasant Town
333-444-5555

Notes:

– State upfront why you are writing and exactly what you support.
– Establish connection to the editorial, story, letter or op-ed you are responding to (if any).
– Offer one or two fresh pieces of information; don't repeat what has already appeared.
– If relevant, tell readers how they can get more information and what they can do.
– Include your name, postal mail address, and phone number for verification.

Letter #2: Opposing a position

Dear Editor:

I am writing in response to your recent story, "Flexible Height Restrictions Called 'Recipe for Visual Pollution.' " Opponents of this change in the zoning code were quoted as saying that it would lead to an unsightly, overcrowded streetscape.

In fact, flexible restrictions would have the opposite result: By allowing some builders to add height instead of depth, we will preserve green space on city streets. This will create a more open, attractive commercial center beneficial to businesses and citizens alike.

Flexible restrictions are also an economic development tool. Other towns that have made this zoning change report increased occupancy rates and higher rents in downtown districts.

I encourage readers to learn more by attending the mayor's public forum on May 10.

Fred Smith
Smith Realty
1 First Street, Pleasant Town
333-444-5555

Notes:

– State upfront who or what you are opposing.
– Explain briefly why your opponent (someone quoted in a story, another letter writer, an editorial writer) is wrong.
– Make one or two key arguments in favor of your position.
– Do not be defensive, combative, or nasty.
– If relevant, tell readers how they can get more information or what they can do.
– Include your name, postal mail address, and phone number for verification.

OP-ED

Like municipalities of similar size all over the state, Pleasant Town is suffering from an economic downturn. We are losing small businesses and failing to attract new investment. At the same time, our downtown streetscape has steadily lost open space and visual integrity.

Now we have an opportunity to address all of these problems at once. Mayor Brown's proposal for flexible building height restrictions would be an economic development tool as well as a way to preserve urban green space. It would benefit both residents and businesses. It has been endorsed by the chamber of commerce, the Realtors Association, the Downtown Retail Board, and Citizens for Livable Urban Communities.

The current ban on all buildings with more than three stories is counterproductive. Instead of creating architectural harmony, it has led to discordance. Because builders could not add height, they created structures that were low but disproportionately deep. For an example of this problem, look at the awkward condominiums on Nice Street.

As footprints grow wider, they also consume more and more green space. Crowded streets are unattractive and unhealthy. A recent survey conducted by the chamber of commerce found that people spend twice as much time shopping in districts with small parks as in dense, overbuilt areas.

Critics of this proposal claim that it will make Pleasant Town less competitive because it will be less unique. In fact, it is the current policy that leaves us unable to compete. When local employers want to expand in place, they are blocked unless their buildings can be widened. Many, like Good Company, have decided it was easier to move somewhere else. For the same reason, new businesses hesitate to invest here and potential residents have fewer local job opportunities. Chamber of commerce data show that towns with flexible height restrictions enjoy commercial occupancy rates and downtown rents significantly higher than ours.

Do not believe the naysayers. Instead, look at the evidence yourself—both on the chamber of commerce website, www.pleasanttownchamber .com, and on the streets of Pleasant Town.

Notes:

– Make three or four clear points instead of many vague arguments.
– Use concrete examples and provide context for your facts.

- Keep your focus local; the publication is not looking for national columnists.
- If you are refuting a specific claim, use specific information.
- Every publication has its own op-ed length limit; if you exceed it, be prepared for your submission to be cut (or rejected).

REGULATORY COMMENTS

(can be adapted to either a written form or as oral testimony)

Comment #1: Opposing a Rule that Would Have a Disproportionate Impact on Small Businesses

My name is Fred Smith. I am the owner of Smith's Family Swim Place in Pleasant Town. Thank you for allowing me to testify against the proposed rule to prohibit a commercial pool facility from hiring any full time employee who lacks a lifeguard certification.

I understand and agree with the intent of the rule, to ensure that someone with lifesaving skills is always on the premises whenever a pool is open. But it would impose an unfair burden on small fitness clubs like mine, where the only full-time employees are administrative staff. Because our pool hours are limited, we hire certified swim instructors and lifeguards only to work part-time.

Instead of furthering the goal of pool safety, this rule would force us to waste thousands of dollars training people who do not interact with swimmers. Those extra costs could cause us to lay off staff or cut pool hours.

I respectfully ask that you rescind this proposal, or provide an alternative for small businesses. For example, I would not object to a requirement that my certified instructors undergo annual refresher training.

I am pleased to answer any questions, or to provide additional information that might be helpful.

Notes:

- Be specific about the impact you oppose.
- Offer a constructive alternative.

- Assuming you agree with the intent of the rule, say so.
- Offer to answer questions or provide more information.
- If you are attending a public hearing, bring enough hard copies of your testimony for each official (and for the media, if you hope to attract press attention).

Comment #2: Supporting a Rule to Ameliorate the Unintended Consequences of an Existing Regulation

My name is Fred Smith. I am the owner of Smith Realty in Pleasant Town. Thank you for allowing me to testify in favor of the proposal to change the city zoning code, providing for exemptions from height restrictions on commercial structures.

When the current restrictions were introduced, the goal was to preserve the visual integrity and historic character of downtown neighborhoods. In practice, however, we have ended up with buildings that are low but disproportionately deep. There is structural discordance instead of harmony, defeating the original purpose. Another unintended consequence is the disappearance of urban green space.

By removing the current ban on any building with more than three stories and substituting a case-by-case evaluation of height plans, this proposal will help to beautify our commercial district. Flexible height restrictions are also a proven economic development tool: They encourage local businesses to expand in place instead of moving to other towns. I urge you to read this report issued by the chamber of commerce, showing that flexible restrictions are associated with increased occupancy rates and higher rents in downtown districts.

I am pleased to answer any questions, or to provide additional information that might be helpful.

Notes:

- Be specific about the unintended consequences of the regulation.
- Explain the benefits of changing the regulation. If you have documentation (like the chamber of commerce report in this example), bring it.
- In a case where you do not agree with the proposed amelioration, offer a constructive alternative.
- Offer to answer questions or to provide more information.
- Bring enough hard copies of your testimony (and any supporting documents) for each public official and for the media.

Comment #3: Opposing a Rule that Is Applied Inconsistently or Arbitrarily

My name is Fred Smith. I am a licensed architect with Pleasant Town Architectural Services. Thank you for allowing me to testify against the current process for getting a waiver from setback requirements.

In my experience, this process results in inconsistent decisions. Having designed several buildings for clients under existing rules, I have seen setback waivers denied on shopping streets where they make the most sense, but granted in residential areas with little justification. This frustrates commercial builders, hinders economic development, and does nothing to protect the visual integrity of Pleasant Town.

Here is the problem: Decisions are based on an applicant's documentation of "reasonable" alternatives. As an architect, I know that some applicants are far more sophisticated than others about what constitutes a "reasonable" design. In effect, you are punishing people for lacking specialized knowledge. Also, members of the Zoning Board may have different opinions about what is "reasonable" in a given area.

The solution is to provide a clear, objective definition of alternatives that would be acceptable in each zone. By including specific guidelines in the code and making them available online, you would eliminate much of the current frustration and boost both commercial and residential construction.

I am pleased to answer any questions, or to provide additional information that might be helpful.

Notes:

- If you have a professional certification relevant to the issue, cite it.
- Be specific about the inconsistency or arbitrariness you have experienced.
- Explain what damage results from the inconsistency or arbitrariness.
- Offer a constructive alternative.
- Offer to answer questions or provide more information.
- Bring enough copies of your testimony for each public official and for the media.

Glossary

Abuse of office   An action taken (or not taken) by a public servant to obtain financial benefit for himself, a family member, or a business associate.

Agenda   An official list of topics to be considered at a particular meeting of a public body.

Appropriation   A legislative act that commits funds to specific programs.

At-large election   An election in which candidates are elected by voters from throughout the jurisdiction, instead of from smaller districts (often called *wards*) within the jurisdiction.

Bicameral   A legislative body with two chambers.

Building code   Local and/or state regulations setting limits on what can be built in a given jurisdiction.

Caucus   A group of legislators or other political (usually partisan) officials to discuss shared policy and/or political interests.

Central business district   A high-density commercial zone.

Chair of county commission   County official who runs meetings and generally oversees the administration of county government.

City council   The policymaking body elected by the voters of a municipality.

City manager   A professional administrator with day-to-day responsibility for all municipal operations.

Civil service   The merit-based personnel system developed to reduce the influence of politics in government hiring and promotion.

Commission   A form of government that combines legislative and executive functions in one body.

Conflict of interest   The ethical problem caused when a public servant may personally benefit from taking or not taking an official action.

Consent agenda   A list of routine or non-controversial topics that can be approved by a public body in one motion, instead of being voted on separately.

Continuance   The postponement of a public hearing or court case.

Council-manager   A form of government in which an elected body has legislative powers, and a professional manager has executive/administrative powers.

County administrator   A professional administrator with day-to-day responsibility for all county operations.

County executive   In some county governments, this is an elected mayor-like chief executive.

Disclosure   The practice of making public, in some form, an official's personal and/or campaign finance records.

Eminent domain   The right of government to seize private property for a compelling public use.

Executive session   A meeting of a public body closed to the public and generally used to discuss litigation or personnel matters.

General election   A popular vote on candidates for elective office (as opposed to a primary election for candidates who will run in a general election).

Gift   An item of value received by a public official without consideration of equal or greater value.

Gratuity   Compensation for the actions of a public official unrelated to government salary or benefits.

Housing code   Local rules for maintenance of residential buildings by land-lords.

Impact fee   Cost assessed against developers to fund infrastructure improvements related to or necessitated by their projects.

Initiative   A question placed on the ballot as a result of citizen petition. Successful initiatives may force legislation, or be non-binding expressions of popular will, depending on state and local law.

Land use regulations   A set of plans and codes related to zoning, building, housing, and other uses of land in a jurisdiction.

Legislative calendar   An agenda or other type of listing of all bills or resolutions scheduled for consideration by a legislative committee or chamber.

Nonpartisan election   Election where candidates cannot officially associate with a political party.

Ordinance   A local law (as distinct from a state statute).

Party boss The head of a political "machine," a highly disciplined party organization with significant power in its jurisdiction.

Party convention A gathering of political party delegates to set policy and/or choose candidates for elective office.

Party primary Elections where voters choose candidates to represent the party in a general election.

Political action committee Commonly known as a *PAC*, this is a fundraising organization designed to make political contributions on behalf of an interest group.

Precinct The basic unit of the electoral process; precincts typically have their own polling places and political party or campaign representatives.

Public notice Government bodies are required to "notice," or inform, the public in advance of their meetings and potential decisions.

Public record Any record, in any physical (and increasingly, online) form, that is retained by a government entity and open to inspection.

Recusal The act of a public official who voluntarily refrains from a vote due to a perceived or actual conflict of interest.

Referendum A ballot item introduced by citizen petition, usually intended to reverse a law passed by the legislature. Like initiatives, referenda may also be non-binding expressions of popular will.

Resolution An statement of intent and/or opinion by a government body.

Rule-making authority The power of a regulatory agency to issue legally binding "rules," or procedural guidelines.

Statute A state law (as distinct from a local ordinance).

Strong mayor A local elected mayor with broad executive and administrative powers.

Sunset provision An automatic expiration date provided for in some state laws.

Turnout The proportion of eligible voters who vote in a given election.

Variance An exemption from zoning regulations, granted on a case-by-case basis by a local review board.

Weak mayor A local elected mayor with limited powers, particularly in budgetary and hiring matters.

Whistle-blowing Public disclosure of information, usually by a government employee, that suggests wrongdoing by officials or agencies.

Zoning Local regulation of the use of property to oversee and enforce compatible development.

Index

About the Author

Assemblywoman AMY H. HANDLIN, PhD, currently serves as deputy minority leader of the New Jersey General Assembly. She is also an associate professor in the Department of Management and Marketing at Monmouth University. Her experience in public office spans 20 years and multiple levels of state and local government. She holds a BA from Harvard, an MBA from Columbia, and a PhD from New York University's Stern School of Business. Assemblywoman Handlin is also the author of *Be Your Own Lobbyist: How to Give Your Small Business Big Clout with State and Local Government* (Praeger 2010).